Focusing 2 Finish

21 Day Inspirational Journey

Cassandra Moye

Printed in the United States of America

Copyright © 2022 Cassandra Moye

ISBN: 9798833670941

All rights reserved. Without limiting the
rights under the copyright reserved above, no part of this publication may be
reproduced, stored in, or introduced into a retrieval system, or transmitted in
any form or by any means (electronic, mechanical, photocopying, recording, or
otherwise) without prior written permission.

Scripture quotations marked "KJV" are taken from the Holy Bible, King James Version (Public Domain).
All rights reserved.

Contents

Dedication		1
1. Day 1 Created		5
2. Day 2 Called		9
3. Day 3 Chosen		13
4. Day 4 Accountability: The New Journey		17
5. Day 5 Pure Intentions- GREATNESS		21
6. Day 6 It's In Your Hands, USE IT!		25
7. Day 7 Everyone Cannot Go- Release and Receive		29
8. Day 8 Clean YOUR Windshields		33

9. Day 9   37
    It's A Love Thing/ Lifting You Higher

10. Day 10   41
    YOUR Conversations: Expectations

11. Day 11   45
    No Trust, No Truth: Boss Up FINALLY TRUSTING YOURSELF!!!

12. Day 12   49
    A Moment In Time, Be Still

13. Day 13   53
    The Covenant: Signed, Sealed, & Delivered

14. Day 14   57
    Oil TOO Expensive, Time TOO Valuable

15. Day 15   63
    The Mountain Experiences, It Is Written

16. Day 16   69
    Own Your Power- Reassurance

17. Day 17   73
    A Chosen Essential Worker

18. Day 18   77
    Living Your Kingdom Life Unapologetically

19. Day 19   81
    Anchored In Self-Care & Self- Love

20. Day 20   85
    Serving The Nations Gratitude

21. Day 21   89
    Purpose, Not Performance

DEDICATION

First and foremost I dedicate this MASTERPIECE back to the Trinity, creator of all, our Heavenly Father GOD, our Lord and Savior JESUS CHRIST, and the HOLY SPIRIT whom is our guide and comforter, for giving me the wisdom to write and entrusting me with such an AMAZING gift I really did not think I had to complete this assignment.

To my King, friend, and phenomenal love, Tim, thank you for holding my hand, praying for and with me, and pushing and believing in me.

To my beautiful, precious children, Robert, Chelsea, Patrick, Gabriel, Hannah, and Caleb, along with my grandchildren Haylee, Trinity, Peighton, MiKayla, Patrick Jr., Audrey, Mari, and Paxton, and my godchildren Brittney and Willie who all believed in me and pushed me to complete this assignment in their excitement to read it after watching me stay up many late nights along with some tearful moments of not understanding why I was crying. I pray they will understand it better by and by, as they evolve into the anointed kingdom building young men and women birthing their gift(s) by answering the call upon their lives.

A heartfelt thank you to my loving, supportive parents, Betty Lewis and Lt. Calvin Dawson, Sr., and my bonus mother Maggie Dawson, for you are the wings beneath my wings. Although my father is not here to witness this moment in time, I believe this is the conversation we had prior to him transitioning from this earthly home. The prayers he prayed upon my life that God was going to use me for His glory are coming to pass.

My phenomenal Godparents, Dr. Raymond and Hattie Polite, for your unconditional love and equipping me under your powerful, anointed spiritual leadership.

My wonderful village of aunts and uncles who helped raised me, Mamie Fulmore, Leonard Fulmore, Anita Tunstall, Retired GyMsgt. Narvin Tunstall.

My praying grandparents, Elnora Fulmore, Annie L. Dawson, J.D. Dawson.

My fifteen amazing siblings, my outstanding godmothers, Patricia Nelson, and Deborah Stewart, my trustworthy BFFs, Patrina Anderson, Alfredia Drummer, Na'Kesha Williams, and Earea Woodson for your love, prayers, and support along my life's journey.

Sitting under the anointed and powerful leadership of Pastor Beau Adams, his beautiful wife Mrs. Kim Adams, and our Community Bible Church family who kept me inspired to live my best life through the teachings the Word of God.

To my God sent angels who have helped me in completing some of the many God-given assignments for my life, Prince Carter, Kimberly Chapman, Evangelist Beverly Broadus Greene(Spiritual Mother), JosCynthia Mason, Commissioner Felecia Franklin, Pastor Sammie Haynes, Nikki Nycole, Yolanda Atwater-Nixon, Robbie Ray, Leann Foster, Ebony Porter-Ike, Annette Swift, and Adrienne Manuel, thank you. I know for certain we have been connected through divinity. Each of you saw the calling upon my life with and with outstretched arms and an open heart you allowed me onto such AMAZING platforms entrusted to you by God. You allowed me to share my gifts with the world. You prayed with and for me, loved me unconditionally, and watered seeds of greatness in my life.

Equally important, I cannot forget to give God praise and a special thank you to the anointed woman of God, Ms. Paula Foster, CEO/Founder of Speak Life Publications, who helped me give birth to this written vision.

To all who have added value to my life, know your generosity of prayers, support, and love have not gone unnoticed. I greatly appreciate and love each of you the same.

PREFACE

Who are you and what do you do for a living are the most asked questions by people we meet along life's journey either to YOU or about YOU to someone connected to YOU. Yet there's more to us than who we are and what we do for a living. This 21-day journal is going to aide you in knowing who you are and whose you are in Christ.

We have all been challenged at a time in our life to accept a developmental change through a 21-day challenge. It may have come in the form of fasting, praying, reading God's Word daily, writing in your journal, not eating out, changing your diet, or even withholding from spending unnecessarily. Scientific research, along with a written article entitled *Personal Excellence,* written by Celestine Chua, shows us the difficulty of embarking on and accomplishing a new habit based on the age old belief of change happening in 21 days. While beginning a new habit can be difficult, the reward is great.

As you begin the next 21 days of cultivating who you have been created, called, and chosen to be, keep in mind that while this new habit of accepting who you are may be difficult in the beginning, the person you are to become is worth the initial hard times. As you go forth *Focusing 2 Finish* your God-given assignments, remember life is a time clock. One day your clock will stop. With everything going on in the world today, do not be dismayed or lose sight of your journey. Keep soaring to higher heights and deeper depths not being anxious for anything with your eyes kept on the prize which is Jesus Christ. One day you will finish your race in first place with a Crown of Glory waiting for **YOU**.

Day 1

CREATED

Today is the beginning and the greatest day of the rest of your life!

The question often asked as we travel this journey called life is, "Who are you?" Because only you can answer this question, one must realize it is not your accomplishments or failures in life that completes you. The reason you were created in your mother's womb was to fulfill God's plans for HIS glory on this earth through the gifts and talents residing within you. Sharing your testimony of the many obstacles and joys on your journey to your set destination will forever change the lives of people and generations scheduled for a divine appointment by the great physician, God, with you.

I'm reminded of hearing people say, "You are JUST like your mother. You are JUST like your father". I'm not saying this is a bad thing, however it is not the truth. You have similarities, yet you are not the same. Each of us has our own identity equipped with different assignments to be completed through our lives. Therefore, you must know you are not your mother or father. They were the chosen vessels to bring you into this world. They were the chosen vessel to birth a powerful seed who would one day go on to water seeds of greatness in the lives of many people near and far. It is time to set yourself free and soar into your destiny.

A lot of people never find the person God created them to be because they are distracted listening to everyone else tell them who they are or what they should be doing. They're also trying to live up to other people's expectations while wasting priceless time creating themselves into the image of what another person they admire or envy thought or said. Yes there are those sent to your life to aide you in your development, however we must know who we are to be rightfully guided in the direction of our destiny. Nevertheless, when such a disease stagnates the seed, it prevents the tree of life, you, from being able to make the impact YOU were scheduled to make. It also becomes confusing when you really do not know who you are. Therefore, do not allow anyone to be the Center of Disease Control in your life. When you come into the knowledge of knowing who and whose you are, you become the spiritual CDC, Claiming Deliverance from Chaos. You hold the antidote. You become the tree of life others feast upon, giving them medicine of healing, hope, love, faith, and wisdom to discover who they truly are. For that reason, your life is the mustard seed of faith which will bring about a big change and a big influence, with an impact others will search for. Their seek will lead them to your tree of life which creates a source they can feast upon, assisting them with the proper nutrients needed to create a God-centered dynamic life. Creation is a powerful gift, which undervalued, has been entrusted to you. The gift of creation provides you the ability to help others walk in their purpose which will bear fruit in the lives they touch.

As I sit here writing, looking out across the mountaintops of God's beauty, gratefulness fills my soul and heart that He took time to create me. He trusted me enough to instill His gifts and talents for the upbuilding of the Kingdom and the world. Why is that you ask? On July 25, 1995 at 7:30 a.m. I was hit by an 18-wheeler carrying gasoline. It caused me to suffer many injuries, including having to learn to walk again with the assistance of many medical devices. Jesus saved my soul. The enemy came in and TRIED to steal, kill, and destroy it. While overcoming those injuries, realizing God had a major plan for my life, I was still looking through the lens of my own eyes not accepting who I was created to be on the earth. Situations kept coming and finally one day, in the process of having to face life and take responsibility for the challenges I'd encountered, I took a stand to humble myself and surrender to GOD realizing HE is in complete control of my being. I, Cassandra Ewings- Moye, knew I was a powerful seed of inspiration, hope, life, change, and love created for God's glory. However, I had to keep moving forward knowing, not by my own persuasion, but my knowledge of God's Word.

When we were created and planted on this earth, we were given the ability to live an abundant life for dynamic change and transformation. Now you are an "EXCLUSIVE LIMITED SUPPLY"!

- Do you know why you were created?
- How are you going to stop the chaos in your life after attempting to live up to other's expectations?
- What tree of life are you?
- What seeds of greatness reside within you?
- Where will you begin to plant your seeds?

Scriptures

Before, I formed thee in the belly I knew thee; and before thou camest forth out of the womb I sanctified thee, and ordained thee a prophet unto the nations. (Jeremiah 1:5 KJV)

The thief cometh not, but for to steal, kill, and to destroy: I am come that they may have life, and that they may have it more abundantly.(John 10:10 KJV)

For we are GOD'S masterpiece he has created is a new Christ Jesus, so we can do the good things he planned for us long ago. (Ephesians 2:10 KJV)

Another parable put He forth unto them saying, "The kingdom of heaven is like to a grain of mustard seed, which a man took and sowed in his field. Which indeed is the least of all seeds, but when it is grown, it is the greatest among herbs, and becometh a tree, so that the birds of the air come and lodge in the branches thereof". (Matthew 13:31-32 KJV)

For this cause we also, since the day we heard it do not cease to pray for you, and to desire that ye might be filled with the knowledge of his will in all wisdom and spiritual understanding. That ye might walk worthy of the Lord unto all pleasing, being fruitful in every good work and increasing in the knowledge of God. (Colossians 1: 9-10 KJV)

Famous Quote

"I was once afraid of people saying, "Who does she think she is?" Now, I have the courage to stand and say. "This is WHO I AM!"

Oprah Winfrey

Favorite Songs

Smokie Norful- *Dear God*

Bethel Music- *All Of My Life You Have Been Faithful*

Leeland- *Way Maker*

Teddy Pendergass- *Wake Up Everybody*

Day 2

CALLED

The telephone is ringing... have you answered the call?

Whether connected to you biologically or through divine appointments, the call on your life will forever change your life, the life of your children, and generations to come. Once you answer the call there will be times when thoughts and feelings of doubt will try to surface. For myself, along with others I've had conversations with, we all experienced moments of thinking we were not worthy of the calling. Fear tried to enter in as opportunities kept coming. I would ask myself if this was really my life and what had I done to be favored with such AMAZING opportunities. I had not done anything heinous or out of character in my life, however the deal breaker for me was when people who knew me would bring up something negative I'd done. It would put me in a place of wanting to check them right quick in an aggressive way, but I had to remember in that moment not to lose who I was evolving into and why I answered my call. Nevertheless, I'm forever grateful they remembered those times in my life as it showed my growth and maturity that continued to help me soar into my purpose. Please do not get dismayed when this happens to you, just as it did for each of us. Prepare yourself whole heartedly. When you answer the call people are going to do the same to you. At this stage there is an urgency and responsibility to release the blame factor which could and/or has sabotaged your life. When things go wrong, which it will, it is a part of our process. Blaming others and harboring unforgiveness will have you in the clinches of folly, causing you to be powerless. You will not be able to change anything around you or create your legacy. It will further cause your relationships to suffer tremendously whether interpersonal, friendships, acquaintances, or romantic relationships and will negatively affect your positive influence on others and yourself. I'm not saying don't get things off your heart and talk about it, but learn to examine both parts in what happened, forgive, and use that story as a step into your destiny and a branch on your tree of life. This will eliminate both stress and mental related illnesses according to the Mayo Clinic Overview. Often those suffering from either one or both ailments often battle with depression, anxiety, decreased appetite, enjoyment of life, problems with drugs and alcohol, detachment from reality, withdrawal from family and friends, and significant tiredness just to name a few. By answering the call on your life, it will cause you to rely on God more aiding in the decrease of the above-mentioned ailments. It places our faith in Him and not man.

Growing up I was in an unstable environment. I was home with my mother until five years of age, then I went to live with my Aunt Mamie and Uncle Leonard for five years. I returned to live with my mother for about four years and off to live with my grandmother Elnora, Aunt Anita, and Uncle Narvin, and finally living with my mother again until I moved out after having my son. It was what it was. I saw my mother on weekends because she worked during the week. I saw my father nearly every day as he was a police officer patrolling our communities and he would stop by to check on me. No matter where I lived it didn't stop the support I had. There most definitely was a village of people who loved and nurtured me into the BEAUTIFUL lady I am today. One of my Aunt Mamie's favorite soap operas, we watched with her as children, was Days Of Our Lives. I still remember the voice of the great announcer, Ed Prentiss, speaking over the instrumental theme: "Like the sands through the hourglass, so are the Days Of Our Lives. In the view of that, no matter what circumstances we face, life continues to go without any time for procrastination.

Many people, young and old, use the excuse of blaming others for their shortcomings of never accomplishing who they have been created, called, and chosen to be. They also harbor unforgiveness towards who did not raise them, those who were not there, those who abused them, even their divorce. Some simply did not do what needed to be done to complete an assignment. Guess what? It does not matter. It was already written in the plans for your journey. GET OVER IT! Stop blaming them or your circumstances, giving them power over your life. This keeps you in a weak position of being controlled by your past and disempowered to not answer your call, simply because you think you must do whatever they tell you to do. You are enslaved to a master who damages your infrastructure of hearing God's call upon your life. Fantasia Barrino sings it all so well in her rendition of Dennis Reed's song, It Was Necessary. What would have happened if I didn't answer my call and continued to live in guilt, shame, and unforgiveness to name a few? Well, you wouldn't be receiving the guidance you need through this book.

Ready to answer the call of God on your life? Great! Now you must let of go of all anger, malice, rage, slander, and abusive language from your mouth and heart. The word of God says in Proverbs 4:23,"for out of the abundance of the heart the mouth speaks". It goes on to say in Proverbs 10:11, "Keep your heart with all vigilance for from it flows the springs of life." Forgiving those who have hurt you, abused you, lied on and to you, stole from you, left you, and betrayed you is sometimes the hardest thing to do, but understand God has something better waiting for you. Remember the forgiveness is not for them. It's for you! Now, most importantly, you must forgive yourself. Forgive yourself for holding on to those things which so easily beset you. Forgive yourself for not knowing. Forgive yourself for making decisions based on what appeared to be love, what appeared to be trust, and what appeared to be wisdom. There is nothing you can do to change it, but everything you can do to change you. Understand without a doubt God is in control. He knows your name, gifts, talents, and the lives you will empower for His glory to change the world for all humankind.

The telephone is ringing, answer your call.

- Do you know what your call is?
- What have you been called to do?
- How are you going to be intentionally to answer the call every day?

Scriptures

Let all bitterness, wrath, and anger, and clamor, and evil speaking be put away for you, with all malice. And be ye kind one to another, tenderhearted, forgiving one another, even for God for Christ's sake hath forgiven you. (Ephesians 4:31-32 KJV)

And we know all things work together for the good to them that love God, to them who are the called according to his purpose. (Romans 8:28 KJV)

Created in me a clean heart, O God; and renew a right spirit within me. Cast me not away from thy presence and take not thy holy spirit from me. Restore unto me the joy of thy salvation and uphold me with thy free spirit. (Psalm 51:10-12 KJV)

Famous Quote

"It's not an easy journey to get to a place where you forgive people. But it is such a powerful place, because it frees you."

Tyler Perry

Favorite Songs

Tasha Cobbs- Leonard-*You Know My Name*

You Raise Me Up-*Josh Groban*

Mary J. Blige-*Just Fine*

Day 3

CHOSEN

Now that you know you are created, called, chosen, and destined for greatness to reign in this life, prepare to live without regrets, allowing humility to step in replacing arrogance. Prepare to live courageously, knowing your true self and being empowered like never before. This only happen when you can answer this question: Will you say yes to God's perfect plans for your life with your words, heart, and soul?

The question people often asked me, and I have asked God, spiritual and community leaders, family members, friends and myself is how do I get there after saying YES? Well, it is simple. First and foremost, commit to the Lord whatever you do, and He will establish your plans (Proverbs 16:3). Next, be faithful over what HE gives you to do. Lastly, keep working on who you are and who you have been chosen to become will begin to be birthed. It sounds easy, however, just as I have faced warfare, so will you, especially saying yes to your call. Anything worth having is worth fighting for and YOU were worth it! That is why Jesus came down and gave His life for YOU! It is not always going to be someone there to pick you up when you fall on the track. Stay focused on the call and remember who is leading you. The mandate of being created, called, and chosen comes without repentance. Stay associated and connected to someone who has the wisdom, knowledge, and understanding of where God is taking you. Every student needs a teacher/mentor. It's not based on race, creed, color, or gender. They need to be equally yoked in your beliefs and truly walking out their mandate.

Every day I speak and listen to positive affirmations of individuals who are sharing their life's journey along with testimonies on how challenging the process was leading up to living their best life now. They include, but are not limited to Pastor Beau Adams, Pastor of Community Bible Church in Stockbridge, GA, Oprah Winfrey, Steve Harvey, Evangelist Beverly Broadus-Green, mother of Snoop Dogg, who prayed for me and spoke a life-changing word over my life, Bishop T.D. Jakes, and Tyler Perry. I follow their sound instructions of what it takes to get to their plateau of sacrifice and their level of service which lead to their success. It's helped me stay focused on becoming who God has chosen me to be. God promises us all success. He does not favor one more than the other. If we live obedient, according to His word in Deuteronomy 28:1-14, we will see the blessings spring forth in our lives.

When I finally made the conscious decision of accepting I had been chosen, it was as if I was standing on the edge of a giant precipice at the top of the mountain taking a leap of faith trusting God. This then caused me to trust myself not to retreat to my comfortable life of working a seven to four job every day which was unfulfilling to my purpose. Your decision will transform your future, introducing you to others who have said yes.

Chosen one: Will you say yes?

Scriptures

For many are called, but few are chosen. (Matthew 22:14 KJV)

But you are a chosen race, a royal priesthood, a holy nation, a people for his own possession, that you may proclaim the excellences of him who called you out of darkness into the marvelous light. (1Peter 2:9 KJV)

You did not chose me, but I choose you and appointed you that should go and bear fruit and that your fruit should abide, so that whatever you ask the Father in my name, he may give it to you. (John 15:16 KJV)

Famous Quote

"I don't condemn anyone for making their choices. If someone chooses those roles, fine. But not for me. When someone stops me and says. You're the reason I became an actress that lets me know I made the right decision."

Cicely Tyson

Favorite Songs

Anthony Brown-*Worth*

Jill Scott- *Golden*

Shekinah Glory-*Yes*

Day 4

Accountability: The New Journey

It is an AMAZING new day on this journey!

What a change that has taken place in your life. With the decision made to answer the call, accountability will play an important part in your life. You will need an accountability partner. What is that? An accountability partner is a person who coaches another one in terms of helping the other person keep a commitment. They help hold you responsible. They won't complete the assignment for you, they will push you through it. There will be assignments you will have to complete on your own. It's during those assignments you must remember the gift(s) residing within you, what your mentor has taught you, and you have the instructions coming from the Holy Spirit. Therefore, your accountability is key and a time for you to B.O.S.S. U.P. BOSS UP is an acronym for:

B- Building

O- On

S- Super

S- Strength

U- Understanding

P- Process

Luke 12:48 tells us to whom much is given, from Him much will be required, meaning you are held responsible for what you have. The assignment upon your life is not for everyone to give you directions or answers, but surely for you to have an accountability partner/mentor who guides you along the way. This person is one who holds you accountable to God's standards for your life. This individual prays with and for you, listens without judging, not always having the answers, yet lending a helping hand as God leads, and pushes you until the assignment is completed satisfactorily. Those who starve with you shall eat with you.

One of my favorite childhood stories is The Little Red Hen. She had such a tremendous assignment on her life. This assignment would allow her friends the ability to eat and be merry. Their only requirement was to help work the vision. She was required to complete several tasks to complete a vision which seemingly needed an entire village of vision workers. That is how it is in your calling. We need a team, those who will guide the vision while holding us accountable, yet we sometimes have too many of the wrong people around us. When God is elevating you into your purpose these individuals will not be able to till the grounds with you and work the vision. Habakkuk 2:1-3 says, "I will stand upon my watch, and set me upon the tower, and will watch to see what he will say unto me, and what I shall answer when I am reproved. And the Lord answered me, and said, Write the vision and make it plain upon tables, that he may run that readeth it. For the vision is yet for an appointed time but at the end it shall speak, and not lie; though it tarry, wait for it; because it will surely come, it will not tarry". As you walk in the vision God has given you, every family member or friend will not be able to accompany you. Why? Some are still holding on to the you they knew yesterday, others aren't there to work the vision, and others can't see and/or understand the vision. They want the benefits. We often look to family and friends to be the first to support us, but there are times they discount what God has guided you in completing. Strangers on the other hand see you as hope, faith, love, and goals. You're giving them the endurance to complete their journey. For this reason, know there will be some family and friends who support you, yet your vision is for an audience greater than them. It will be those who see greater in you who will be your accountability partners and run with the vision assisting you in completing this part of your journey. It will be those who see greater in you who will be able to run with the vision.

Although The Little Red Hen was a fictional story, it gave us insight of what comes with preparation and the work of a God-given vision. When she realized she had to build on her faith and God-given promises no matter how challenging it was, she found herself, just like you may at times, planting seeds in the fields with super strength, not giving up simply because she understood the process and therefore you must too. She was given a vision and she gave it back to God. Therefore she needed vision runners. We find out along life's journey our goals never change, the plan to get there may and that's okay. God will send you vision runners who can and sometimes will double as your accountability partners. They will be the ones who make sure your goals are being completed while keeping you covered in prayer. With that understanding, your great expected end, which is to carry out the vision God has given you, cannot be done to the level of excellence without an accountability partner.

- Who is/are your accountability partner(s)?
- Can you think of five people who you can reach out to asking them to be your accountability partner? Not that you need all five, moreover so you will have options which is a key component in keeping your endurance strong while on this journey.

Remember you cannot do it by yourself. God has divine appointments setup for you to meet the right people at the designated time. Sometimes you will have to walk this journey alone. At times there may not be an accountability partner walking with you hand in hand. This is where the teacher is silent. God will allow certain tests and trials in your life sending different people to help you through it along the way. Understand some of your accountability partners are seasonal. They don't all stay for the entire journey as some are only qualified to get you through a season. Honor the ones who have entered your life whether it is just for a day, a month, a year, or a couple years. Do not be afraid to share the truth with them around your needs, desires, and even areas you are lacking in. If you cannot trust them with your assignment, they are not an option to hold you accountable. No matter what type of accountability partner you need, a key factor I learned listening to comedian Steve Harvey was that of the wisdom given by his mom during a s season of his life. She said, "Son you do not have because you do not ask God". James 4:3 says, 'When you ask, you do not receive, because you ask with wrong motives, that you may spend what you get on your pleasures". When choosing an accountability partner(s) make sure you pray about it and if necessary fast about it. You want to ensure those on the team are in alignment with the assignment of who you have been created, called, and chosen to become.

Scriptures

By wisdom a house is built, And by understanding it is established. (Proverbs 24:3 KJV)

Every one of us will give an account of himself to GOD. (Romans 14:12 KJV)

The Lord says, "I will guide you along the best pathway for your life. I will advise you and watch over you. (Psalm 32:8 KJV)

And the Lord said to me, "Arise go on your journey at the head of the people, so that they may go in and possess the land, which I swore to their fathers to give them. (Deuteronomy 10:11 KJV)

Guard through the Holy Spirit who dwells in us the treasure which has been entrusted to you. (2 Timothy 1:14 KJV)

He who tends the fig tree sill eat it's fruit, And he who cares for his master will be honored. (Proverbs 27:18 KJV)

According to the glorious gospel of the blessed God, with which I have been entrusted. (1 Timothy 1:11 KJV)

Famous Quote

"YOU cannot leave what's important to YOU up to someone else".

Steve Harvey

Favorite Songs

William Murphy- *You Reign*

Mary J. Blige- *My Life*

Day 5

Pure Intentions- Greatness

HEART POSTURE

Greatness is priceless! It's not accompanied by discounts or mark downs. You need to make sure everything attached to YOU is of pure intentions. It is day five of YOUR journey. By now there should be a stirring in YOUR soul preparing the next dimension of YOUR life to get in position for the assignment God has prepared upon YOU. Everyone has an assignment to complete in their lifetime. However, your assignment requires you to have no ulterior motives or comparison to someone else's gift(s) and the life they are living. A pure heart produces pure intentions which opens doors for your gifts to be utilized to serve others. Your assignments and gifts are not for personal gain, yet they are for Kingdom gain. You have been anointed for the assignment to be a blessing to the called generation assigned to you.

I guess YOU are wondering why this topic was included on this journey. Both pure intentions and greatness are principals of strength linked with success. Let us take a walk with the word pure. I've created an acronym for P.U.R.E. It is:

- Purposely
- Understanding
- Reasons for
- Excellence

It is important for one to realize the seriousness of being pure, along with the heart posture. When it is not postured properly the gifts are used on as needed basis because the gifts come without repentance. At times it might look the same, but God will use whomever He pleases to deliver a message or a word. That person may not realize they are being used by God. The gift is still there, but the heart is not in a pure enough place to be used to the extent God wants to use them. Therefore daily we all must pray to clean our heart and renew the right spirit within us.

Relationships of every kind are important on this life's journey. The reasons behind why we get involved in those relationships are what makes the difference. Think back to a friendship you once had, a relationship you entered, a ministry you joined, or a job you started working. Were these relationships started from a pure place of wanting them or a need for the moment to fill a void in your life? It is the same effect with your gift(s). From the least to the greatest of your actions, it must be from a pure place to link you to excellence in your journey. Be careful not to allow anyone to tell you differently because it will cause you to sway in many unnecessary directions. You MUST be careful who is in your ear giving direction on your decisions. If you are not discerning or have the wisdom to see the enemy using them, it can and will take you out of the pure place causing you not to operate in excellence. You MUST pray and ask God to awaken your spirit of discernment, giving you the ability to decipher who is really with you and those who are against you. Don't over indulge, giving too much attention to who it is. Know who they are, but don't allow them to take your mind and heart away from what God is calling you to do. There will always be those sent to taint your purity and it begins by securing your trust.

Have you ever been around a person who was negative all the time no matter where you all were or what was going on? Or maybe you've dealt with people who intentionally brought you around those they knew you did not affiliate with nor did they affiliate with you? A lack of pure intentions sometimes shows up is an individual's lack of concern for your boundaries. It also shows up when dealing with selfish people or those who are not being loyal to the team, only showing up when it is beneficial for them, or not appreciating everything given and all being poured into them. Be sure your intentions are right and you are submitting all things to the Father before adding anyone to your circle.

Prince Carter, my God sent Angel and colleague, asked me how I would know when a person's intention are not pure. After a few minutes of allowing the question to marinate, I began to think back in my life. My initial reaction was to make sure I was in the correct heart posture to answer the question truthfully with no animosity. Nevertheless, based on my life's experience I realized the warning signs were always there, but I chose to ignore them. While coming to understand MY intentions were impure as well. How? The person's gift, at least I thought, was a part of the vision given and necessary to move the team forward. However instead of me seeing the true purpose of the individual, I focused on my needs and vision at the time. It was not until later, after the team was moving forward, I began to see the true intentions of their heart. Had I submitted the individual to God before allowing them on the team, the distractions and delayed time would have been avoided. This would have also caused me to do a heart check before bringing them on the team. Sometimes our excitement for the vision causes us to unintentionally become selfish and leave God out. All we see is the vision.

We're all guilty of being extremely excited about a vision and temporarily having an impure heart. Yet allow me to help you so you don't make the same errors. A lack of pure intentions sometimes shows up as one talking bad about everyone else, something always not being right about someone else, not being loyal to the team, only showing up when it is beneficial for them, or not appreciating everything given and all poured into them. Be sure your intentions are right and you are submitting all things to the Father before adding anyone to your circle. This will ensure your heart's posture is correct as well. By submitting the vision and the intended team members or those you are seeking to add to your circle, you will not have operated from an impure place of wanting that person to stay a part of the team only because it benefits the vision. Our experiences are going to be different with people whether with pure intentions or not, yet we'll all have relatable topics and warning signs to be discussed to share with others.

Remember your excellence is tied to your pure intentions because God is speaking to us every day.

- TRUST YOUR GUT FEELING ESPECIALLY WHEN YOU ARE GOING BACK AND FORTH WITHIN YOURSELF.
- DO NOT TRY TO FULFILL FLESHLY DESIRES.
- GRAB HOLD OF WHAT THE HOLY SPIRIT IS TELLING YOU.

As my grandmother Elnora would say "If a person is no good to YOU, they ain't going to be no darn good for you." Having pure intentions is the source of excellence that occupies your mere existence advancing YOU to success.

Scriptures

Create in me a clean heart, O GOD and renew a right spirit within me. (Psalm 51:10 KJV)

All the ways of a man are pure in his own eyes, but the LORD weighs the spirit. (Proverbs 16:2 KJV)

Do two walk together, unless they have agreed to meet? (Amos 3:3 KJV)

For where your heart is there will your treasure be also. (Luke 12:34 KJV)

Famous Quote

"Once YOU have confidence in your instincts, YOU must never allow other people's refusal to believe, or their data to refute, what YOU know instinctively is true".

Bishop T.D. Jakes

Favorite Songs

DeLeon Sheffield- *Hands*

Micah Stampley -*The Corinthian Song*

The Color Purple- *God Is Trying to Tell You Something*

Fantasia Barrino- *Feel Beautiful*

Bill Withers- *Lovely Day*

Day 6

It's In Your Hands, USE IT!

It is empowering to know your future is in your hands.

There are many times we hear people make excuses around what they do not have. They complain saying, "If I was like so and so my life would be so much better. Then all my dreams would come true". If you really knew the behind the scenes struggles of that person's life YOU would be thunderstruck looking at your situation. All so often we see the glitz and glam of an individual's life portrayed on social media, television, and even someone we may encounter daily at work, church, or in the community. This puts people in a frenzy of thinking they do not or cannot measure up to the level of a person who may have the same gift(s) as them. But what YOU may not understand is they had to start somewhere as well. They took the initiative by stepping out on faith, trusting what they had in their hands. Therefore, when YOU started this journey you probably did not think you had much to offer. However, at this given time take a moment, look around you and access the inventory you have in your hands. This includes your gifts, resources, and relationships of people who are willing to offer an open door of opportunities for you to share what you have in your hands. Thus allowing your gifts to make room for you.

It's empowering to know God has entrusted me. He's entrusted me on red carpets to interview celebrities, to speak at empowerment events to youth groups, even to have my own show. This trust brought about an evolutionary change not only in my life, but the life of others through working the covenant principals with what has been placed in my hands. Just as God has done for others, HE will do the same for you. I'm reminded of the story of Moses in the book of Exodus, chapter 4.

God asked Moses what was in his hands. Moses thought it was a staff, but to God it was an instrument capable of performing miracles. It parted the Red Sea and it brought water out of the rock. Moses didn't know what he truly possessed in his hand, yet God did. There will be times when it is not always easy to identify what's in your hands because of situations sent to distract and stagnate your vision. Yet God still knows and will not allow you to miss it. In view of the fact that one's thought of how everything will turn out, one must be humble and teachable by a leader with sound insight and wisdom, not being sidetrack by other people's opinions of what you have and how it should be used. In some circumstances people will try to control the outcome of your GOD given plans, not completely surrendering to GOD allowing Him to direct them ensuring what is expected of you unfolds the written plans for your life along with redefining your life's journey.

I met a young man six years ago in Atlanta, Georgia by the name Prince Carter. He shared his story with me of resigning from his job, packing up and leaving Baltimore, Maryland with a few belongings headed to Atlanta with $14.67 in his pocket. He slept in the train station bathrooms until he found somewhere to live, working odd end jobs. He didn't quite know or understand why God sent him to Atlanta when he did, but he knew GOD had a major plan for his life. Although Prince had all of that going on in his life, he knew his assignment was to start his own media company sharing inspirational interviews. He used what he had in his hands, the gifts of branding and marketing. He then reached out, offering an open door of opportunities for others who were likeminded with the tenacity of building a media team. Six years later many of the original team are still there sharing their gifts of videography, photography, journalism, craft services, wardrobe styling, and makeup. Others served diligently for a season and moved on. I'm not saying quit your job and pack up and move, but in everything get understanding. Following GOD'S directions for your journey will not be the same as his. All of our gifts require a different level of faith and obedience. Our testimonies may relate, but our journeys will not be the same.

The same illustration is for YOU. Whatever gifts God has placed in YOUR hands, no matter how insignificant YOU may think it is, whatever YOU withhold and retain in YOUR HANDS reveals what is in YOUR heart. God is waiting patiently for YOU to offer the gifts to others and back unto him. YOU ONLY HAVE ONE LIFE TO LIVE ON THIS SIDE. THERE IS NOT ANOTHER ONE FOLDED IN THE DRAWER OR HANGING IN THE CLOSET. Trust GOD completely with what He has given you and watch the manifestation of His promises of blessings in your life. What is in your hands you are not using? What do you have in your hands already to fulfill your call in the earth? Today stop and begin using what's in your hands to evolve from where you are in order to make a pivotal mark in the earth empowering people. Empower those you're called to grasp hold of their future. Help make the world a better place for all humankind to live together.

Scriptures

Let the favor of the Lord our God be upon us, and establish the work of our hands, upon us; yea, the work of our hands establish thou it. (Psalm 90:17 KJV)

Commit thy works unto the LORD, and thy thoughts shall be established. (Proverbs 16:3 KJV)

The LORD will open the heavens, the storehouses of his bounty, to send rain on your land in season and to bless all the work of your hands. You, will lend to many nations but will borrow from none. (Deuteronomy 28:12 KJV)

Famous Quote

"I don't know what you're up against; I don't know what you're facing. But here's what I do know. You've got something special, you got greatness in you, and I know it's possible that you can live your dream."

Les Brown

Favorite Songs

Yolanda Adams- *Open My Heart*

Yolanda Adams- *I'm Gonna Be Ready*

Donald Lawrence & Co.-*Back II Eden*

Diana Ross- *I'm Coming Out*

Day 7

Everyone Cannot Go- Release and Receive

CAN YOU SEE THE DIFFERENCE?

Where you are going everyone can't go. Now is the time for you to understand who is destined for this journey and who is not. Hopefully, as we enter the seventh day, you are more focused and beginning to understand you have been called, created, chosen, and set apart. You've been made aware of the need and importance of having an accountability partner in order to complete the assignment on your life, knowing everything you need is in your hands.

There are five questions I need you to answer today as you are becoming more acquainted with your assignments here on earth. These questions are vital to building your endurance to stay focused and determined to finish this journey without distractions that could delay you.

- Are you starting to see the difference in people's actions around you?
- Are you noticing a change in your competence and awareness?
- Has anyone noticed you are moving into your purpose of who you have been created, called, and chosen to be?
- What and who are you ready to release?
- Are you ready to receive the fresh anointing about to release upon you?

It is AMAZING to me how as I listened to the voice of God while writing this devotional, each day aligned with what needed to happen on that day. The number seven biblically and spiritually means completeness or the end of a thing. As you enter day seven on this twenty-one day Focusing 2 Finish journey, you have now entered the space to release people, places, and things which brought you negative energy, negative words, rejection, and the tangible losses you have endured. Everyone is not entitled to the blessings awaiting you, and some things cannot be attached to you while moving forward in your purpose. This is your place of peace.

Life will bring about distractions because they are inevitable. You are responsible for not allowing them to curtail your life's journey. One of my favorite role models, Oprah Winfrey, whose life is an open book to the world, has allowed us to see the many distractions she endured. She was born into poverty in Mississippi. She became pregnant at the age of 14 and lost her son in infancy. Yet when left in the care of her grandmother, her foundation in God was established. Of course the enemy didn't like that and sent distractions to not only affect her faith, but affect her destiny. From sleeping on porches because of the color of her skin, to abuse from those who were supposed to love her. Yet God stepped in and made a way for her come back. Oprah was sent to live with her father once again in Nashville, Tennessee where her life began to turn around for the good standing on the solid foundation her grandmother gave her as a child. She began speaking in church, writing speeches that produced an income, working at local radio stations while still in high school, became a college graduate, and co-anchored at a local television station which went from a third rated to FIRST! NOW THAT'S THE DIFFERENCE!!! Nevertheless, it did not come without many distractions for Oprah. She held on to her faith in God. Even in her darkest moments she knew this too would pass. By and by, when the morning came she would be able to tell her story as she released those who had hurt her and received the promises of God knowing that troubles don't last always.

Focusing 2 Finish is not always easy. You are going to have distractions from people, children, jobs, and life, however in the midst of these occurrences you cannot allow the distractions to cloud your journey. There are people who will start off looking as if they are a part of your journey and they are there to support you, yet slowly, but surely things will begin to change because they are on an assignment to distract you however possible. Sometimes you will distract yourself trying to live your life for someone else and not for yourself. As your purpose continues to evolve others see it and often become intimidated by you, sending distractions to get you off track. Go back to Oprah's beginnings as a co-anchor. After working seven months at Baltimore's WJZ-TV, she was fired and reportedly told by one of the producers she was unfit for television news. We are talking about the world's GREATEST American Host, television producer, actress, author, and philanthropist, who told her Kindergarten teacher she did not belong there because she had such a large vocabulary. How did she go from being promoted to the first grade to being told she was unfit for television news? How was she NOT a fit? This is an example of how a distraction will be sent to attack your purpose. If she would've held on to all that had been done and said to her, Oprah Winfrey would not be who she is today. She would not holds the many positions she does. There were some who started out with her who are no longer with her today. We are talking about the world's GREATEST American Host, television producer, actress, author, and philanthropist. We are talking about THE Oprah Winfrey who told her Kindergarten teacher she did not belong there because she had such a large vocabulary leading to her being promoted to the first grade. She, of all people was told she was unfit for television news. How was she NOT a fit? This is an example of how a distraction will be sent to derail your purpose. If she would've held on to all the negative words spoken to her, Oprah Winfrey would not be who she is today. I believe there were others who saw the greatness upon her life and allowed the views of others to cloud their vision causing the to lose out on an opportunity of a lifetime. An opportunity that could have assisted them in completing a portion of their life's assignment. By and by when the morning came, she was able to tell her story as she released those who hurt her in order to receive the promises of God knowing that troubles don't last always.

As you continue on this journey with a clear vision, becoming aware of your purposed filled journey, recognize and understand distractions will be sent. Do not allow them to cloud your vision. Do not allow them to cause you to miss an opportunity of a lifetime. It is important for you to understand everyone is not entitled to go where you are going. Release them where they are. Release what they said and did to you, continuing to open your mind and heart to endless possibilities Focusing 2 Finish on who you have been created, called, and chosen to become.

Scriptures

Therefore, since we are surrounded by such a great cloud of witnesses, let us throw off everything that hinders and the sin that so easily entangles. And let us run with perseverance the race marked out for us. (Hebrews 12:1 KJV)

I pressed toward the mark for the prize of the high calling of God which is in Christ Jesus. (Philippians 3:14 KJV)

I will instruct you and show you the way to go, with My eye on you, I will give counsel. (Psalm 32:8 KJV)

Walk with the wise and become wise, for a companion of fools suffers harm. (Proverbs 13:20 KJV)

Now Joshua the son of Nun was filled with the spirit of wisdom, for Moses had laid his hands on him; and the sons of Israel listened to him and did as the LORD had commanded Moses. (Deuteronomy 34:9 KJV)

Famous Quote

"I have also found that for myself, since I've had no religious education, it was so interesting to see the different versions of heaven and what life on earth means."

Barbra Walters

Favorite Songs

Hezekiah Walker- *Every Praise*

Beyonce- *Listen*

Louis Armstrong- *What A Wonderful Day*

Day 8

CLEAN YOUR WINDSHIELDS

I CAN SEE CLEARLY NOW!

Now that you understand everyone cannot go with you and you have released and received seeing yourself as God sees you as the righteousness of His son Jesus Christ.

Distractions are on the agenda of life. They are defined as having one's thought or attention drawn away; unable to concentrate or give attention to something. They are intentionally sent to keep you off the assignment. We often let them in the door because we are unaware of what they look like. Distractions range from small occurrences we brush off, to massive ones which began as small ones we ignored in doubt of believing we are being affected by something. Some distractions you are equipped to automatically ignore. You're able to see it for what it is. On the other hand, there are those distractions that come as you are in the middle of your assignment. The enemy then sends a distraction causing you to doubt you are truly on assignment. Understand there's always something or someone the enemy will use to take you off course of what God has ordained in your life.

Distractions are like severe rainstorms as you are driving to your destiny. Instead of allowing situations to blind your view, turn on your I.G.N.O.R.E. wipers. Include God Not withstanding One Ramshackle of an Event.

This means no matter how hard it's raining in your life, applying the scriptures of God, along with the principals lining up with your gift(s), and knowing who is in your circle helps you to come through the distractions. Think back to when we talked about having an accountability partner who should be able to see the danger before it hits. It's during your distraction they should be able to instruct you on how to maneuver through those dangers which hit unexpectedly. Always remember your chosen accountability partner(s) should be able to discern when there is a storm approaching being your vision runner.

Distractions also increase your wisdom. Have you ever experienced a time when it seemed as if every corner you turned there was something there to take you off track? These moments are teaching you how to maneuver in life, overcoming distractions. You will not see the same distraction every time, but you will begin to learn to discern what a distraction is and how to maneuver through life. Think back to five of your most valuable relationships whether they were monogamous, job related, platonic, a friendship, or ministry. Every relationship was not the same. Some enhanced you, while others drained you. Those which drained you, what was going on in your life to cause you to miss the small signs of the distraction growing? Once you realized it was a distraction and overcame it, how did you apply it to your life? Those are the moments you were taught distractions will come when you are in the midst of your mission showing you how to protect the assignment, increasing your discernment. Those moments gave you a keen sense of knowing when distractions are about to surface and the different levels and access points of distractions. Within those five relationships it gave you the ability to formulate healthy relationships, not settling for anything less than what it takes to complete your assignment. This also gave you the will power to fight through and not be affected by the distractions as much.

As you grow in life, when the distractions come, they will be like water running off your back. You will know what it is and be able to immediately rebuke or get rid of it. You will know how to survive through the rainstorms. Remember the lessons you learn through each distraction, while knowing each distraction is to ultimately help you complete the assignment, cultivating you in your walk with God. Not all distractions are tedious, however they all work out for the glory of the Kingdom of God. God redirects you the entire time.

I am reminded of a story written by Andrew Jobling of a father and his teenage daughter driving home after spending a day out together. The daughter was learning to drive at the time and needed to practice, so she asked her father if she could drive. Being a loving and encouraging father, he said ABSOLUTELY. They stopped the car and swapped seats. Her father was impressed by how attentive and skillful his daughter was. After driving a distance, a storm was approaching and the daughter started to feel nervous, asking her father whether they needed to pull over and wait for the storm to pass. Her father looked at her and said, "No we'll be fine, keep driving". And because her father said so, with reassurance she kept driving. It was not long before they were in the eye of the storm with strong wind blowing, hard rain with limited visibility in front of them, clashes of thunder and lightning and she told her father she was scared asking him once again if they should pull over because all the other cars were pulling over. Once again in his still calm voice he said no keep on driving through the storm. Soon after they were through the storm. The rain stopped, the wind eased, and the sun started to break through the clouds. The daughter was visibly shaken by what she experienced, but relieved and proud of herself, regaining her focus. She turned and looked at her father asking him, 'Why did we keep driving through the storm dad, when stopping seemed to be the safer thing to do?" The loving father requested that she stop the car. They pulled over and stepped out of the car, looked back along the road they had just travelled, and the storm they had just come through. He asked his precious daughter, "Where are all those people who stopped?" She looked puzzled, shrugging her shoulders and said, "Back there somewhere in the storm." "Yes," her father replied. "They stopped and so they are still in the storm and will be stuck there longer. We kept driving and we made it out to the other side.

When enduring distractions, it is imperative to know who is in your circle. When they are the right people, they'll be able to do just as the father mentioned above did his daughter, not allow you to stop just because it's storming. They'll be willing to endure the storm with you. These individuals will be very honest with you. Sometimes your feelings maybe hurt but take a moment to hear what they are saying before you react. When you are divinely connected to people who want to see you win, they will be there up and through the completion of their assignment with you.

As you continue this miraculous journey, remember storms are inevitable and necessary. As long as you have your I.G.N.O.R.E wipers on, you will be fine. The Word of God instructs us, eye hath not seen, nor ear heard, nor have entered into the heart of man, the things which God hath prepared for them that love him. (1 Corinthians 2:9) Stay the course as you learn to maneuver through the distractions and you'll be singing, "I Can See Clearly Now the Rain Is Gone".

Scriptures

Finally brethren, whatsoever things are true, whatsoever things are honest, whatsoever things are just, whatsoever things are pure, whatsoever things are lovely, whatsoever things are of good report, if there be any virtue, and if there be any praise, think on these things. (Philippians 4:8 KJV)

I can do all things through Christ which strengtheneth me. (Philippians 4:13 KJV)

The LORD is my shepherd; I shall not want. He maketh me to lie down green pastures: he leadeth me besides the still waters. He restoreth my soul: he leadeth me in the paths of righteousness for his name's sake. Yea, though I walk through the valley of the shadow of death, I will fear no evil: for thou art with me; thy rod and thy staff they comfort me. Thou preparest a table before me in the presence of mine enemies: thou anointest my head with oil; my cup runneth over. Surely goodness and mercy shall follow me all the days of my life: and I will dwell in the house of the Lord forever. (Psalm 23 KJV)

No weapon that is formed against thee shall prosper, and every tongue that shall rise up against thee in judgment thou shalt be condemn. This is the heritage of the servants of the LORD, and their righteousness is of me, saith the LORD. (Isaiah 54:17 KJV)

Famous Quote

"Your results are the product of either personal focus or personal distractions. The choice is yours."

John Di Lemme

Favorite Songs

Tamela Mann- *Step Aside*

Michael Jackson- *Man in the Mirror*

Johnny Nash- *I Can See Clearly Now*

Day 9

It's A Love Thing/ Lifting You Higher

BEING IN LOVE IS A BEAUTIFUL THING!!!

It's truly a love thing. YOU have endured such a breathtaking journey serving unconditionally using the gifts given to you from creation. You have been pouring into others not understanding they were gifts GOD had for a selective audience. When you are willing to go and serve without questions or monetary gain, regardless of the audience, it's fueled by love and love alone. When you know your purpose is to inspire, to illuminate, to ignite the souls shifting atmospheres, nothing else matters except the love for God's call on your life. Your call should bring about a difference wherever you go. People should be able to look at you and know certain things can't be said or done in your presence because of the unwillingness to compromise. They should see the set standards of your gift(s) observing he/she is the one not to be played with when it comes to the Kingdom and serving people. You might still be wondering how this is a love thing. Love affects the calling. God loved you so much He created, called, and chose you appointing your gift(s). These gifts will be used to pour into others in a loving manner no matter how people treat you. You still must love as GOD loved. In doing so you will inspire, shift atmospheres, and set Kingdom standards. Regardless of the mantle upon your life, you have to do it in love. Remember Jesus had Judas and He did not cast him away because he had a purpose in the earth. Jesus loved him even when He knew he was going to betray him. Many of us who have been called to do something great will experience betrayal and there is no getting around not having a Judas in your camp. Keep that Judas close to you and love him/her regardless. Now that you have answered the call you have to walk this thing out in love. You will be backstabbed, talked about, ideas taken from you, and people will use you for their benefit, yet THAT'S WHY IT'S A LOVE THING!!!

When there is someone or something you love so dearly you will nurture and give it all you have within you to make sure it is protected and well taken care of. If you are a parent who is reading this book, you will understand what I'm about to say. Although it wasn't planned, the discovery at the Jacksonville MEPS (Military Entrance Processing Command) at the tender age of seventeen, my senior year of high school, I was told I was about to be a mother. At first I was so angry with myself because I thought my life was over. I was trying to figure out how I was going to tell my father, my mom, my Aunt Nita, and Uncle Narvin I was pregnant. So many thoughts came to my mind. Either I was going have an abortion and enlist in the Army or give birth to a precious baby who did not ask to come here. It took me about three weeks to tell my father I messed up. Here I was thinking he was going to be angry with me, but his response was, "I already knew. I was praying for you while waiting for YOU to tell me I'm going to be a granddaddy." Whew!!! What a relief that was! It made it so much easier to tell everyone else. As time went on I began experiencing such a love beyond measures for the precious little boy(a gift) growing on the inside of me preparing to make his grand debut into the world. Now that's LOVE.

When God has given you a gift(s) the expectation is for you to love what you have been called, created, and chosen to do without regrets nor wanting to abort the mission. Regardless of what others may deem necessary or unnecessary for your mantle, they, nor you, have the blueprint for your life. God is the only one who holds the blueprint and has given you these gifts. Love the gift(s) without idolizing your mantle. Even more, love the people you are serving more than the gift. The world has and is changing because YOU love who you are becoming! That's A Love Thing!

Scriptures

Each of you should use whatever gift you have received to serve others, as faithful stewards of God's grace in its various forms. If anyone speaks, they should do so as one who speaks the very words of God. If anyone serves they should do so with strength the God provides, so that in all things God may be praised through Jesus

Christ. To him be the glory and the power forever and ever. Amen (1 Peter:10-11 KJV)

For by the grace given me I say to every one of you: Do not think of yourself more highly than you ought, but rather think of yourself with sober judgment, in accordance with the faith God has distributed to each of you. For just as each of us has one body with many members, and these members do not all have the same function. So in Christ we, though many, form one body, and each member belongs to all the others. We have different gifts according to the grace given to each of us. If your gift is prophesying then prophesy accordance to your faith; if it is serving then serve, if it is teaching then teach: if it is to encourage, then give encouragement if is giving then give generously; if it is to lead, do it diligently; if it is to show mercy; do it cheerfully. (Romans 12:3-8 KJV)

You are the light of the world. A town built on a hill cannot be hidden. Neither do people light a lamp and put it under a bowl. Instead they put it on its stand, and it gives light to everyone in the house. In the same way, let your light shine before others, that they may see your good deeds and glorify your Father in heaven. (Matthew 5:14-16 KJV)

Famous Quote

"Career should be a spiritual pursuit not just a physical or financial one. Your career should be where your dreams, aspirations, talents, and hopes for the present and future play out."

DeVon Franklin

Favorite Songs

Ricky Dillard & New G- *Amazing*

Hezekiah Walker- *Grateful*

Jackie Wilson- *Your Love Keeps Lifting Me Higher and Higher*

Day 10

YOUR CONVERSATIONS: EXPECTATIONS

YOUR CONVERSATION MATTERS!!!

There is something POWERFUL about a conversation. Whether it's positive or negative, words have the magnetic force to attract whatever YOU say which leads to YOUR actions and what others around YOU will do. Nevertheless, being on day ten of YOUR Focusing 2 Finish journey, there are three questions to ask YOURSELF. Only YOU hold the answers. How should my conversations differ now than before? Who should I be conversing with? What should I expect from the conversations that are being conducted?

As I sat writing this inspirational masterpiece, I began to reflect upon a time in my life when I decided not to allow any conversation to part my lips, not giving life to the people surrounding me nor myself. Once you decide to be a spring of living water, out of your heart will flow the necessities to make your gift(s) effective throughout the world. This will not only capture the heart and ear of the Father, it will allow you to be invited to many tables and platforms to share productive conversations with those of influence who are educating, equipping, and empowering lives of this generation and generations hereafter. Be aware not to allow anyone's conversations, expectations, or deadlines push you away from becoming the greatest version of YOURSELF. Allow God to set your pace and enjoy the life lessons of the gift(s) within.

Throughout life your conversations will always matter. They will reveal your character, honor, and integrity. They will help you form partnerships and friendships along the way. There may be times you disagree, but that's okay. It not only deepens the connections, it also challenges one to think differently. We have all been raised differently. We all come from different spiritual backgrounds and theology. We all have experienced different paths in life. The expectation of any conversation should always be productive, helping push each other forward and upward in your purpose. The expectation should further be to push each other to another level of comfort and a more in depth concept of the birthing of your gift(s). Always let your conversation be seasoned with salt for it gives flavor to everything you taste. Know how to answer everyone with respect before giving an answer or opinion. Pray before you speak, remembering you are the one who holds the cup that shall overflow with blessings. There is always going to be something you will say which will leave an impression on people's lives that will be spoken throughout many generations. THEREFORE, YOUR CONVERSATION MATTERS!!!

Three questions to answer in your journal today that will always be available for you to reflect on:

1. What conversations bring you fulfillment on this life's journey? Why?
2. What conversations do you prefer not to engage in? How will you separate yourself from it?
3. How will you always allow your conversations to be seasoned with inspiration and importance to others?

Scriptures

Let no man despise thy youth; but be thou an example of the believers, in word, in conversation, in charity, in spirit, in faith, in purity. (1 Timothy 4:12 KJV)

Who is a wise man and endued with knowledge among you? let him show out of good conversation his works with meekness of wisdom. (James 3:13 KJV)

Let your speech always be with grace, as though seasoned with salt, so that you will know how you should respond to each person. (Colossians 4:6 KJV)

Let no unwholesome word proceed from your mouth, but only such a word as is good for edification according to the read of the moment so that it will give grace to those who hear. (Ephesians 4:29 KJV)

Famous Quote

"Speak in such a way that others love to listen to you. Listen in such a way that others love to speak to you."

Anonymous

Favorite Songs

Donnie McClurkin- *I Love To Praise Him*

Fred Hammond And Radical For Christ- *We're Blessed/Shout Unto God(Live)*

Maze featuring Frankie Beverly- *Golden Time Of Day*

Day 11

NO TRUST, NO TRUTH: BOSS UP FINALLY TRUSTING YOURSELF!!!

FINALLY TRUSTING YOURSELF!!!

If you have no trust, you will never have truth in YOUR life.

It is day eleven of this miraculous journey and you have been able to share your truth in all honesty, most importantly with yourself, as well with other like-minded people. As I researched the significance of the number eleven on a spiritual level, it is considered to also define an association of illumination in addition to our inner teacher of enlightenment, creativity, presenting itself to an innovative you. This will refine whatever gift(s) laying within you, propelling you into a powerful leadership position which you have been called to enhance, a better you being able to Boss Up, and not building a level of arrogance always remembering this is Kingdom Work, Level Up, in addition to Word Up owning your truth and trusting your decisions of answering your God given calling.

We as people have the tendency of thinking it takes other people to make us feel worthy of the vocation we have been created, called, and chosen to do. Sometimes in life we find ourselves trusting the wrong people to cultivate us which causes one to walk in a lack of truth and delays us reaching our destiny. Now it is time to take that back. Never forget where you began and who helped you along the way, yet it's time to trust yourself. If you do not trust yourself you cannot walk truthfully in your calling. If you do not trust yourself in your calling, you will shy away from it and delay your season to walk in the power and authority given unto you. God will send the right ones to assist you with your call. Remember they are not God. He's using them to assist you. It was already written in God's plans this would happen. I'm not saying not to be forever grateful with those who assist you during your journey. They were all vital in helping you get to where you are currently. Please don't forget where you came from and who GOD sent to help you become the person HE has called you to be.

Truth be told we all have gone through some trying times in our journey, however iron sharpens iron along the journey with true leaders showing leaders the way to be strong and very courageous. True leaders are not afraid to cultivate you to where you are going, nor are they afraid for you not to be afraid to accept the very aspect of your existence using the power that resonates within you to trust yourself. You know you have been chosen, but along your journey you have been in a place where others have torn you down. This could have come from sitting under toxic leaders, having parents who spoke negativity over your life, or toxic people you came into contact with who intentionally choose to tear you down making you feel as if what you are doing is not good enough. This caused you to go into a spiral of confusion. True leaders will show you how to accept the power resonating within you and to trust yourself even if it is a season of stagnation. For this period of time enjoy the presence of the Trinity(God the Father, God the Son, and the Holy Spirit). This season is pushing you into owning your truth, your life, your character, and your future, purifying your heart of everything preventing growth and ridding it of everything that will prevent the growth of your leadership position. Doing this will allow living waters to flow out of you, saturating all connected to you.

Because your destiny was given to you before being formed in your mother's womb, it is time to Word Up, speaking the oracles of God out of YOUR mouth. Put a praise on it and travel onward, trusting the destination of your journey. When you reach the spoken place in your life, you will reflect on the person you have become. You will realize the gifts you have birthed, the people you have made connections with, and the transitional inner growth that has taken place. It will always be your leaning post whenever in doubt as you continue on this prodigious journey causing YOU to go to the next level.

Scriptures

Now the LORD said unto Abram, Get thee out of thy country, and from thy kindred, and from thy father's house, unto the land I will shew thee: And I will make of thee a great nation, and I will bless thee, and make thy name great; and thou shalt be a blessing. (Genesis 12:1-2 KJV)

And they said unto him, Ask counsel we pray thee of God, that we may know whether our way we which we go shall be prosperous. And the priest said unto them; Go in peace before the Lord is your way wherein ye go. (Judges 18:6 KJV)

For he shall give his angels charge over thee; to keep thee in all of thy ways. (Psalms 91:11 KJV)

A man's heart deviseth his way; but the LORD directeth his step. (Proverbs 9:6 KJV)

Famous Quote

"Just trust yourself then you will know how to live."

Johann Wolfgang von Goethe

Favorite Songs

Chris Tomlin- *Sovereign*

James Fortune- *I Trust In You*

Anthony Brown & FBCG- *All In His Hands*

Charlie Wilson- *I'm Blessed*

Day 12

A Moment In Time, Be Still

STOP AND REFLECT!

Now that you understand the expectations and importance of walking in your truth, it is time to rest in God for further directions on where He is calling you. As you are reading day twelve, we, the world, will forever remember COVID-19. This was a moment in time never to be forgotten for generations to come. It brought people together worldwide of all economic statuses, ethnicities, and faiths. It brought some to repentance, some prayer, some sorrow due to the loss of loved ones, in addition to testimonies of healing and praise. Two months prior, around February 20th, I faced writer's block and did not understand why. I was praying asking God for wisdom concerning topics for the remaining seven chapters of this book. I had an expected release date of April 3, 2020, however nothing would flow. As the days progressed, I took some time to sit and talk with God knowing He would give me instructions and strength for whatever was waiting ahead for me on this journey. The spoken instructions came. They were to keep fighting the good fight of faith and complete the assignments He is giving me without worry because HE HAS ME.

During all this, my Uncle Leonard transitioned from this earthly home. Uncle Leonard was a man who was instrumental in cultivating my life having been raised in the home by he and my Aunt Mamie. They were distinguished people in the community, loving, delivering biblical discipline and prayer during my grade school years. This accredited to the solid foundation I am equipped to stand upon. His passing gave me a moment to reflect on my precious childhood memories and priceless moments well spent with them. It seemed as if the world was standing still. After his passing, there was death after death of dear friends, classmates, ill family members, love ones being quarantined home, while others were hospitalized not knowing if they were going to survive. In the midst of everything going on throughout the nation, it taught me how to "BE STILL", taking time out to reminisce on the good times in life from my childhood to my adult life. It allowed me to spend real time with loved ones in our household eating dinner together at the table, having wholesome family prayer time, and partaking in conversations realizing what really mattered. This brought me to chapter twelve on April 3, 2020 at 3:58 a.m. To GOD be the GLORY for release!!!

Although it seems as if trouble is in the land, whenever you are faced with adversity of any sort "BE STILL"! Do not stop what you have been created, called, and chosen to do. Amid completing our assignment(s) we are faced with being tossed and driven with your daily responsibilities of life. It is imperative to take time and quiet everything around you in order to listen for God's wisdom. During your quiet time, receive His strength, nutrients, and power. This is important. You can't pour from an empty cup. You must be refilled. If you don't take time to get quiet and sit with the Father, you'll be too burned out to focus on completing what you were truly put here in the earth to do.

Be like a tree planted by the still waters allowing God to cultivate you in how He sees fit. No matter what is going on, know YOUR leaf will not wither. Surely obstacles will take place in your life. It may hurt sometimes beyond what words can explain, nevertheless, "BE STILL", allowing Him to prune YOU. Every branch, which consists of people, situations, and things connected to you, no longer serving purpose in your life must be removed. Take time at the end of this day to stop and reflect, enjoying your journey and hearing the voice of God in the stillness of time.

Now that you have realized YOU are a tree yielding fruit which will give others hope and healing,

- How will you be still and hear GOD?
- Where is your quiet place?
- When will you take time to stop and reflect?
- What did you hear GOD say in your stillness of time?

Scriptures

Be still and know that I am God. (Psalm 46:10 KJV)

I am the true vine, and my Father is the husbandman. Every branch in me that beareth not fruit he taketh away: and every branch that beareth fruit, he purgeth it, that it may bring forth more fruit. Now ye are clean through the word which I have spoken unto you. Abide in me, and I in you. As the branch cannot bear fruit of itself, except it abide in the vine; no more can ye, except ye abide in me. I am the vine, ye are the branches; He that abideth in me, and I in him the same bringeth much fruit; for without me ye can do nothing. If a man abide not in me, he is cast forth as a branch, and withered; and men gather them, and cast them into the fire, and they are burned… Ye have not chosen me, but I have chosen you and ordained you, that ye should go and bring forth fruit and that your fruit should remain; that whatsoever ye shall ask of the Father in my name; he may give it you. (John 15:1-6, 16 KJV)

Famous Quote

"In the stillness of your presence you can feel your own formless and timeless reality as the unmanifested life that animates your physical form. You can feel the same life deep within every other human and every other creature. You look beyond the veil of form and separation. This is the realization of oneness. This is love."

Eckhart Tolle

Favorite Songs

Tasha Cobbs Leonard- *Smile (Live)*

Israel and New Breed- *Friend of God*

Mary Mary-*I Can't Give Up*

Vickie Winans- *Safe In His Arms*

Day 13

THE COVENANT: SIGNED, SEALED, & DELIVERED

It Is Signing Day!

Have YOU ever been in a place where everything was going well and under control and all of a sudden BOOM, everything around you became chaotic and a sudden shift took place? Well, it is day thirteen and what you may be sensing or experiencing today, I do not know. What I do know is, everything is under control. You are the miracle predestined for today. You have been signed, sealed, and delivered to share your God given gift(s) and testimony with the world. The number thirteen has many different meanings. The meaning we will identify with is the biblical and prophetic meaning of this POWERFUL number. Thirteen is associated with the suffering of our Lord and Savior JESUS CHRIST. Because you were created, called, and chosen by the Almighty GOD, this is equal to what you'll experience or have begun to experience. The sufferings and trials you have endured along your life's journey has brought you to this destination of traveling twenty-one days of FOCUSING 2 FINISH your God given assignments.

One of the world's greatest musicians, who, born prematurely, being placed in an incubator with too much oxygen, becoming blind at the innocent and pure age of six weeks old, is none other than the artistic, brilliant, dynamic, handsome, powerful, resilient, suave', Mr. Stevie Wonder. He taught himself how to play the harmonica at five years old, the drums by eight years old, and in 1961 Stevie was discovered by his friend Gerald White. Gerald asked his brother, American

Musician and co-founder of The Miracles, Ronnie White, to come and hear little Stevie play and sing. Ronnie White in return introduced Stevie to Berry Gordy of Motown Records who was not impressed by his singing or playing the drums, but the sound of the harmonica being played by this blind 11-year-old little boy is what captured the heart and ears of Berry Gordy. Won't He, GOD, do it? By the age of twenty Stevie wrote and released the song which resonates with the young, middle, and seasoned generations, making us dance and sing today, "Signed, Sealed, Delivered I'm Yours". Stevie played many instruments and was strongly involved in the church. Despite the obstacles he was faced with he kept going. With that level of determination he won 25 Grammy Awards! What a signed covenant life to live.

There is a story to be told behind everything you do. Therefore, Stevie's deed was signed and sealed pushing Stevie to deliver because he said, "JESUS I AM YOURS! Yes to your will, way, and written plans for my life." It is written! There is a legal deed of purchase for your spiritual house signed by the Almighty. Your acknowledgement of who He is, obedience of following the principles of God, and for your faithful work, you are that house JESUS said; "That thou are _____YOUR NAME_____, upon this rock I will build my church and the gates of hell shall not prevail against it" (Matthew 16:18). The sufferings and hardships of rejection, depression, hate, fear, guilt, divorce, and molestation, for example, do not live in YOUR house anymore. Not saying you are exempt from any sufferings of hardships, however they are necessary for obtaining the SEALED paperwork. For it is written, "that ye have suffered a while make you perfect, stablish, strengthen, settle you"(1 Peter 5:10). Whereas you have endured some trials and tribulations, even in the process, it's working for your good. It's part of your building and cultivation because everything comes with a price.

"For it is written you have asked and received, sought and found, knocked now it is open (Matthew 7:8), DELIVERED unto you a new home with open doors of opportunities to be a powerful, effective leader sharing your gift(s) throughout the world. Know everything is under God's control. You have been signed, sealed, and delivered!!! I challenge you to answer the following questions:

- What is your story?
- What covenant have you asked GOD for?
- What are you expecting GOD to fulfill for you?
- Are you willingly to endure and stay in obedience for your signed and sealed covenant to be delivered to you?

Scriptures

When anxiety was great within me, your consolation brought joy to my soul. (Psalm 94:19 KJV)

I know your deeds. See, I have placed before you an open door, that no one can shut. I know that you have a little strength, yet you have kept my word and have not denied my name. (Revelation 3:8 KJV)

Famous Quote

"In three words I can sum up everything I've learned about life; It goes on."

Robert Frost

Favorite Songs

Josh Baldwin-*Stand In Your Love*

Tasha Cobb Leonard- *Sense It*

Stevie Wonder- *Signed Sealed Delivered (I'm Yours)*

Day 14

Oil Too Expensive, Time Too Valuable

UNDERSTAND THE COST

CeCe Winans sings it all so well in her song, Alabaster Box.

Now that you understand the expectation and see the importance of being still, the covenant has been signed, giving you authority to go to the next level. You have captivated your boldness to live with no regrets, silencing the voices of people who didn't understand the calling upon your life, singing with a voice of triumph, and working diligently in the lives of people you have been called to serve. God's Word instructs us to use our time wisely, herewith teaching us to number our days because there are going to be situations sent to distract you. Keep in mind you must stay the course not knowing what today nor what the future entails for your life. It costs too much to waste your time. Be confident in knowing the baton has been extended to you and God has exalted you higher. He has anointed you with fresh oil, enabling you to walk in your power, living with a greater purpose in this world. As a result of knowing your time is too valuable and your oil is too expensive to waste on situations beyond your control, and the pettiness of anyone not adding value to your life's purpose, you must be in the company of people of the same mindset who recognize the oil and the assignment on your life. You may not have the same paths, yet your journeys will be in alignment. They are confident in knowing you all can finish the race and don't mind being there for you as you are there for them. As my sister Patrina loved to hear me say… "THAT PART". Continue to keep in mind your time and oil is valuable regardless of people thinking, feeling, or saying you have changed. Be so confident in your calling you know who to invest your time and oil in because everyone is not going to be receptive of the calling on your life.

Upon writing this book, when the time came to publish it I was not quite sure of who would travel this part of the journey with me. I fasted and prayed asking God to send the right publishing company and person(s) who would not only publish, but share their journey with me, including the world as well. He did just that! Oh what a journey and it's been all good!!! In the process of editing, Ms. Paula Foster, founder of Speak Life Publications who wears the garments of owning several businesses, gave and prioritized her valuable time to pour her expensive oil on me in other areas of birthing the gifts in my life along with this book. Over the course of enjoying this part of the journey, I was graced with opportunity of Ms. Paula Foster sharing parts of her journey with me in birthing many gifts and the assignments she is called to complete in the world. During the process of birthing this masterpiece I was instructed to share life stories of people who I've met along my journey who could be written as a reverence piece for the readers. I asked if I could use her journey to share, and she accepted. There were seven important questions I asked Ms. Foster that assisted me in sharing a portion of her journey. In discussing her understanding of the oil on her life, she now understands becoming a woman of virtue, along with the costs of her time and oil God has so richly entrusted her with, must conjointly be applied to your daily life as you complete this race. In the process of owning several businesses, being a mother, grandmother, ministry leader, coach, publisher, and enlarging her territory, Ms. Paula counted the cost of her oil recently. After being married for two years, she began to see the value of her oil and applied that value to everything she does going forward as she runs her race. She understands it is important to prioritize and manage your time to bring balance in order to capitalize on your gift(s) daily. She knew in the midst of birthing her gift(s) and the demands of daily living, both equally important, when time is not managed you aren't managed. This will cause you to fall behind and waste time leaving you unprepared for what's to come in all areas of your life. After accepting the call upon her life, obstacles surely joined her on the journey. That put her in a place of pouring her expensive oil upon people who did not value her oil leaving the evidence of being drained until she was empty. Ms. Paula knew it wasn't good balance of not having enough oil when she needed it. Because of the unselfishness of pouring out to others in their time of need, it shows her love for doing what God has called her to do, yet an imbalance of valuing her time and oil. Although her heart's desire is to always be there for everyone and meet their expectations, she concluded, after facing many obstacles, everyone is not worthy of her time or oil. Knowing who and where to pour is very important. Doing so into the wrong people was not adding value to her day or life. Ms. Paula owns a publishing company, a coaching academy, and other businesses where she assists others in giving birth to the gift(s) residing within them. During the course of pushing people to live a purposeful life, she found some people took advantage of her time and calling while pulling without following sound instructions or insights. That's when she had to back away. There will come a time on your journey where you will have to do likewise. We all experienced something in 2020, whether good, bad, or indifferent. Not that Ms. Paula did not know it, but sometimes we all must come to this place in life, just as the POWERFUL Publisher Paula Foster. She had a great awakening realizing if she does not honor her time no-one else will. Therefore, with a completely made-up mind and heart, she is utilizing her oil and time Focused 2 Finishing her race by seeking God first before she pours into anyone or any project. Also, by knowing who God has called her to be unapologetically, it enables her to have a healthy balance and finish strong.

Even Jesus valued his time and oil. He knew who was important to Him. Think of the story where he was sitting teaching a group of his disciples in the city of Capernaum and someone said to Jesus, "Your mother and brother are outside wanting to speak with you." His response was, "Who is my mother and who are my brothers?" Pointing to his disciples He said, "Here are my mother and brothers. For whoever does the will of my Father in heaven is my brother, and sister, and mother." Therefore as you journey onward doing the will of the Father, prioritize your time of pouring your oil upon the ones eager to learn from you as they birth their gifts and proclaim their purpose in the earth to accomplish God's perfect plans.

There are eight questions I would like to leave with you as you go throughout today to answer. I hope they will add value to your life:

1. Why do you think it is important to prioritize and manage your time?
2. How important is your time to you?
3. Is everyone worthy of your time? If so to what degree?
4. Have you counted the cost of your oil?
5. What did your oil cost you?
6. What obstacles did you encounter where you had to pour out your oil? What were the results?
7. What made you finally realize your time is too valuable and your oil is too expensive to waste?
8. How are you going to use your time and oil FOCUSING 2 FINISH your race?

Scriptures

Walk in wisdom toward them that are without, redeeming the time. Let your speech be always with grace, seasoned with salt, that ye may know how ye ought to answer every man. (Colossians 4:5-6 KJV)

To everything there is a season, and a time to every purpose under the heaven. A time to be born and a time to die, a time to plant, and a time to pluck up that which is planted. A time to kill, and a time to heal, a time to break down, and a time to build up; A time to weep, and a time to laugh, a time to mourn, and a time to dance; A time to cast away stones, and a time to gather stones together, a time to embrace, and a time to refrain from embracing; A time to get, and a time to lose; a time to keep, and a time to cast away; A time to rend, a time to sew, a time to keep silence, and a time to speak; A time to love, and a time to hate; a time of war, and a time of peace, What profit he that worketh in that wherein he laboureth? (Ecclesiastes 3:1-9 KJV)

I have found David my servant; with my holy oil have I anointed him. With whom my hand shall be established mine arm also shall strengthen him. The enemy shall not exact upon him; nor the son of wickedness afflict him. And I will bear down his foes before is face, and plague them that hate him. But my faithfulness and my mercy shall be with him; and in my name shall his horn be exalted. (Psalm 89:20-24 KJV)

But my horn shalt thou exalt like the horn of an unicorn: I shall be anointed with fresh oil. (Psalm 92:10 KJV)

Let us not become weary in doing good; for at the proper time we will reap a harvest if we do not give up. (Galatians 6:9 KJV)

Famous Quote

"Time is free, but it's priceless, YOU can't own it but YOU can use it. YOU can't keep it, but YOU can spend it. Once YOU'VE lost it YOU can never get it back."

Harvey Mackay

Favorite Songs

CeCe Winans- *Alabaster Box*

Joshua Rogers- *Pour Your Oil*

Debra Snipes- *Put Oil In Your Vessel*

Byron Cage- *Breathe*

Tasha Cobbs Leonard- *Gracefully Broken*

Israel & New Breed- *Friend of GOD (Live)*

Earth, Wind, Fire-*Devotion*

Day 15

The Mountain Experiences, It Is Written

A CALL OF DUTY!!!

HOORAH YOU ARE IN THE ARMY OF THE LORD NOW!!!

You are a soldier who has answered the call of duty and accepting it without a shadow of doubt. The climb of the mountains aren't easy and warfare is truly real. The thoughts of fear, doubt, and unbelief will creep in and try to overthrow you on this journey. As it is written, we all will face warfare throughout life's journey. The Bible teaches us of God permitting problems and trials to strengthen our faith, giving us endurance to complete life's race, while drawing closer to HIM. Whatever mountains are in front of you speak to it believing you have the power to move it. These could be mountains of your marriage, children, business, finances, job, or even your walk with Jesus. Most importantly be not afraid because instructions have been given to you for life's victories. Finishing the assignments God has given you, you will face hiccups and roadblocks. You may face trials and obstacles you would have never faced had you not answered the call upon your life. Yet, you are on the cusp of the greatest days of your life. You are there! It is day fifteen and I believe in YOU!!!

I'm reminded of when my baby boy, Patrick, left for basic training after enlisting in the United States Army. I was a proud, but scared mother. Although we had many family members who served in different branches of the armed forces, it was different seeing my baby leave home to serve the country. We knew a great lifetime decision had been made because Patrick answered his call. He was scared and so was I not knowing what was ahead in his new journey. Yet, I knew he was equipped, having been raised in a loving home with biblical principles, knowing the Word of God. He knew how to fast and pray when being faced with any mountain in his life too hard for him to climb. Even if he had to tarry he was prepared. Therefore, after hugging him at MEPS (Military Entrance Processing Station) and seeing him board the van responsible for taking him to be trained for his call to duty, I knew GOD was with and for him. Instantly all my fears left. After completing ten weeks of training, we arrived at Fort Leonard Wood Missouri to celebrate the accomplishment of my son and so many other soldiers. We were alongside other families waiting and watching for them to make their grand entrance as they marched and sung the Army's Cadence (HORRAH) coming around the building. Guess who was leading his company? Our soldier, Private 1st Class, Patrick Moye. After being presented to their families, he greeted us and said to me, "Mama this was the hardest struggle of my life I've had to endure. I wanted to give up because the spirit of doubt tried to overtake me. I was thinking I wasn't going to make it." His heartfelt response was, "But mama thanks be to GOD I made it. Because of your love for me and the biblical principles you taught us, I made it." Oh what a joy to hear your child tell you what a difference you made in their lives. He, along with so many others, completed basic training, answering their call to duty. They went through being torn down mentally, physically, and spiritually. Yet, while going through, they were being cultivated to being educated, equipped, empowered, and prepared soldiers able to defeat any obstacles, gaining endurance to run the race, to be the best they can be to protect and serve. Now that's ARMY STRONG!!! For the reader who is reading this book who has served in any branch of the armed forces THANK YOU for your service and answering your call to duty.

Maybe you did not serve in any branch of the armed forces. There IS another army to serve in. That's GOD'S ARMY! Serve in the kingdom with the gift(s) within you. Just like the natural army, there will be many mountains to climb and warfare to face upon answering your call to duty. It was already written in YOUR blueprint. It was already written the tearing down and rebuilding that would have to take place to design a beautiful masterpiece like YOU to be a fountain of healing and restoration. GOD knew you would need to be able to withstand life's storms in order to give shelter, instructions, and water to others as they go through the storms assigned to their life.

The shelter is the uncompromised word of GOD you to know when facing mountains and warfare once answering your call. Fear does not come to HIM, but rather GOD wants you to walk in HIS power according to 2 Timothy 1:7 KJV. The written instructions are your compass. When in doubt of which way you should go, follow the direction of God confidently knowing you will arrive safely according to Joshua 1:9 KJV. As Mark 11:23 KJV instructs, learn to speak to your mountain. The water hydrates you so you will never thirst again, giving you a productive new life with flowing fountain of words, wisdom, and life. This will wash away all the negative thoughts of not thinking YOU are worthy of YOUR gift(s), asking questions of why me or when will I get my breakthrough, wanting to give up because YOU think it's too hard. There may be times you do not have the money or resources, yet that will not stop you if you continue running your race and singing your "WAR CRY SONG". According to John 4:13-14 lets us know that those who drink the water of the Jesus will never thirst again. When you are dedicated to what you have been called to do, you have to live by faith to reach your destiny. Take a moment to remember three of the most heart wrenching experiences leading up to you answering your call and thinking, "Really? This is where I am?" You felt as if you were at your lowest of lows. You felt as if you weren't going to make. You may have even questioned if you were on the right path. Despite that, remember the victories and growth which came on the other side of the lows. The lows of each mountain you overcame. Whether it was having to sleep in your car, deal with depression, or nights of crying not knowing what to do or where to turn. This may not be your list, however, think of the lows you overcame which you can now call victories. The list may be continuous, yet you pulled yourself up by your bootstraps and got back in the race. It's been and will continue to be imperative on this journey. When you are chosen, realize mountains and warfare are a part of the journey you will enjoy sharing one day. The testimony will be a balm of healing to friends, family members, colleagues, mentees and people all over the world. Keep this thought in the front lobe of YOUR mind at all times: The greatest of the greats have life battles. Why? Because they keep us HUMBLE and before the fountain of God's GRACE. Therefore, no matter where YOU may find yourself in life, no matter what mountain you are faced with in the midst of warfare, remember these are written tests of YOUR faith. The answers are how YOU will suit up, putting on the whole armor of GOD, standing firm on God's promises concerning you, knowing you are the answers to someone's problem. (HOORAH)

There are five questions for you to think about and answer on how this chapter will help you in these areas of your life.

- What area do you keep repeating the test?
- What mountains are you facing right now?
- How will you fight this spiritual warfare and put it to an end?
- What is the area of mentorship you find yourself always helping others in?
- What is your marching song?

Scriptures

Humble yourselves, therefore, under God's mighty hand, that he may lift YOU up in due time. Cast all your anxiety on him because he cares for you. (1 Peter 5:6-7 KJV)

One of your men puts to flight a thousand, for the Lord your God is He who fights for you just as He promised you. (Joshua 23:10 KJV)

He replied, "Because you have so little faith. Truly I tell you if you have faith as small as a mustard seed, you can say to this mountain, Move from here to there', and it will move. Nothing will be impossible for you." (Matthew 17:20 KJV)

The he showed me a river of the water of life clear as crystal, coming from the throne of God and of the Lamb, in the middle of its street. On either side of the river was the tree of life bearing twelve kinds of fruits, yielding its fruit every month, and the leaves of the tree were for the healing of the nations. (Revelation 22:1-2 KJV)

He that believeth on me as the scripture hath said, out his belly shall flow rivers of living water. (John 7:38 KJV)

I returned, and saw under the sun, that the race is not to the swift, not the battle to the strong, neither yet bread to the wise, nor yet riches to me of understanding, nor yet favour to men of skill; but time and chance happeneth to them all. (Ecclesiastes 9:11 KJV)

Famous Quote

"Mountains know secrets we need to learn. That might take time, it might be hard, but if you just hold on long enough, you will find the strength to rise up."

Tyler Knott

Favorite Songs

Yolanda Adams- *In The Midst of It All*

Brooklyn Tabernacle Choir+ - *Sometimes It Takes A Mountain*

Pastor Smokie Norful- *Old School Prayer and Praise*

Brian Courtney- *Worth*

Sounds Of Blackness- *Optimistic*

Survivor- *Eye Of The Tiger*

Kelontae Gavin-*No Ordinary Worship*

Day 16

Own Your Power- Reassurance

The closer you get to finishing an assignment, the uninvited guest, self-doubt, will show up to the celebration. It shows up in the most confident moments, yet it whispers these imputed thoughts in your mind:

- Is anyone going to listen to me?
- Do they even like what I'm doing?
- Am I worthy?
- Am I anointed to do this?
- Am I qualified?
- Am I consecrated enough?
- Do I trust myself to do this?

Despite these thoughts from the enemy, you have a cheerleader in me. I am here praying for you, supporting you, and pushing you. Even though I may never meet you, I am still covering you. Remember everything you need is already within you. Stay in God's presence and own who you answered the call to become without hesitation and without regret. It's already done with reassurance. Because you have stayed in your Bible, stayed in prayer, fasted, and completed your studies, now God can trust you with what He called you to do. You earned the authority in the kingdom. Don't let your hard work go to waste. Own your power by taking your rightful place of authority commanding the Kingdom of God to arise in YOU like a flaming fire. Continue to break barriers, generational curses, overcome obstacles, and grow in YOUR spiritual and natural walk.

You have graduated from a season of average to now dominating every gift lying within you. Therefore it is necessary to watch your eye gates, letting nothing blur your vision or cause you to take your eyes off the prize. It's necessary to guard your ear gates, being careful to hear the right directions to take. Guard your mouth gate not speaking on anything not attached to your purpose. Matthew 12:37 KJV says, "for by thy words thou shalt be justified and by thy words thy shall be condemned." If YOU talk about your doubts, setbacks, losses, and failures you are providing others with a photo album of YOUR life appearing to be a failure. They will never see YOU as a winner. Every time you talk, you are programming yourself and others. Your mind should be conditioned to accept your successes and triumphs. Whether you are a divorcee, experienced bankruptcy, been homeless, gone without a job, etc., a mistake one makes during trying times is speaking negatively about the situation. Winners never do that. I was once both of those people. I learned to wait until the experience passed and shared it as a triumph. Your successful future is set in motion by YOUR words. Winners are people who have birthed their talents, abilities, and special God given gift(s) despite the odds being against them.

I can still hear my father's voice as if it were today sitting in our family room. He would ask us, "Who are YOU?" We all would reply with whom we desired to become. We also talked about our shortcomings and how we could embrace and uplift each other to keep from losing the most important thing in the world, time. When you dominate in your authority you don't focus on the past or focus on the future. You walking in your authority in the moment means standing in obedience with whatever God is giving you at that time. I love the way my father, my hero said it, "My beautiful daughter Cassandra, there is a miracle in YOUR mouth! So continue talking in the direction you want YOUR life to move." He would always leave us with a positive word telling us to reach up, take in, and absorb the beauty of now. There are many blessings of opportunities in the world. How you receive them is totally up to YOU. Equally important, I never thought sitting around with our father would teach me how to dominate my authority in the kingdom enabling me to be able to pass it on to you in this moment. Furthermore, "Own YOUR Power" with reassurance it is YOUR'S for the taking.

- How will you dominate your authority in the kingdom?
- What will you take action towards your purpose and accept the change?
- How do you see your life now since being on this 21-day journey?
- Will you allow yourself to continuously evolve after finishing this book, owning your position and purpose in this world?

Scriptures

For this reason I remind you to fan into the flame the gift of God, which is in you through the laying on of hands. (2 Timothy 1:6 KJV)

That your faith should not stand in the wisdom of men, but in the power of God. (1 Corinthians 2:5 KJV)

God is my strength and power and he maketh my way perfect. (2 Samuel 22:33 KJV)

And behold, I send the promise of my Father upon you; but tarry ye in the city of Jerusalem, until ye endued with power from on high. (Luke 24:49 KJV)

Famous Quote

"Power isn't control at all – power is strength, and giving that strength to others. A leader isn't someone who forces others to make him stronger; a leader is someone willing to give his strength to others that they may have the strength to stand on their own."

Beth Revis

Favorite Songs

Shirley Caesar- *The World Didn't Give It To Me*

Chris Tomlin- *Our God*

Jonathan Nelson- I Believe (Island Medley)

Earth, Wind, & Fire- That's The Way of The World

Day 17

A Chosen Essential Worker

An essential worker is defined as one who is somebody who holds a specialized knowledge whose services are essential for a successful operation of the business enterprise. Such a person could be working for the parent company abroad or just hold certain specialized knowledge/skills. This does not only apply to the business of the world, it applies to the business of the Kingdom.. Any area of being an essential worker is imperative to the kingdom. Whether you are a chef, healthcare worker, police officer, truck driver, cashier, teacher, foster parent, sanitation worker, or Pastor, your work is Kingdom as well. How? The same gifts can be used when working in the vineyard. We use them to encourage and help others transform their life through adhering to their call. In the capacity you are serving and have been chosen to do in the kingdom of God, walk in total obedience by doing what is good and required of you. What does the Lord require of you? To act justly, to love mercifully, and to walk humbly with your God. Because we all have work to do, nobody is nonessential when it comes to your gift(s) being worked in the earth.

It is the seventeenth day and we are on the cusp of this twenty-one-day journey. You are evolving into your God-given power whom you said yes to becoming in order to make this world a better place. You are almost there! Seventeen biblically and spiritually, relates to overcoming the enemy, victory, resurrection, spiritual perfection, and order. When broken down in its simplest form, eight, we know that represents new beginnings. So as you have now begun to own your authority, you are entering into a season of new beginnings where you will overcome the enemy and celebrate the victory. There will be restoration, spiritual perfection, and order coming into your life. Because you are an essential worker this day is symbolic of what is going on in your faith of beginning the journey of who you are. Everything you have done up to this point has been preparing you for the essential work you have to do. Therefore, continue to seek God's wisdom in every area of your life daily, which is your daily bread for each given assignment because you are ESSENTIAL!

There are so many BEAUTIFUL stories to share with you of people who are essential workers who have gone over and beyond to make sure we had the necessities to survive during the pandemic. Mr. Mike, an employee at our local Chick-Fil-A in Lovejoy, GA, who greets everyone with a smile illuminating your soul and kind words making your day better is who comes to mind. My children and I visit the restaurant at least three times a week. Gabriel is always looking for him. He remembers the conversation I had with Mr. Mike where we talked about the work he does and always being there early in the morning ready to serve no matter how bad things were appearing to be in our country. I asked him what brings him so much joy as he never seems to have a bad day. His response was, "I am so blessed to be here and while there are others who we must pray for such as our first responders, I was called to do this. Not only that, I was chosen by God to serve no matter what may come my way. I know I am covered by the blood of Jesus. It also brings me great joy being able to serve meals to families and it gives me hope every time I see a returning or new customer come up to the drive through that it would bring us all closer together in love, making all of us kinder and appreciative of what we have." Just like Mr. Mike, you are leading the way with clarity and using your gift(s) with the purpose of making this world a better place to Live, Laugh, and Love. YOU ARE ESSENTIAL!!!

As you stop and reflect on your surroundings and how you serve others, what a privilege it is to represent the love of Jesus, being granted grace to care for everyone who is around you. You have been given an opportunity of priceless moments and precious memories to bask in, as well to share with others of earthly treasures, serving cultures of families and communities, uplifting and celebrating victories won by the people you serve along life's journey. .WHAT A GREAT HONOR TO BE AN ESSENTIAL WORKER!!!!

Your job title might not be one of the people listed in the beginning of the chapter, but there are two questions I would like to leave with you of how you view the work you render.

Did you ever think of yourself as an essential worker?

How does your journey aligned with the essential work you have been called to do?

Scriptures

For this purpose also I labor, striving according to HIS power, which mightily works within me. (Colossians 1:29 KJV)

So that you will walk in a manner worthy of the Lord, to please Him in all respects, bearing fruit in every good work and increasing in the knowledge of God. (Colossians 1:10 KJV)

A gift opens the way and ushers the giver into the presence of the great. (Proverbs 18:16 KJV)

Let love and faithfulness never leave YOU; bind them around YOUR neck, write them on the tablet of YOUR heart. Then YOU will win favor and a good name in the sight of GOD and man. (Proverbs 3:3-4 KJV)

Do not muzzle an ox while it is treading out the grain, and The worker deserve his wages. (1Timothy 5:18 KJV)

Famous Quote

"Getting to know who you are is the most essential information that you can find our about yourself."

Sunday Adelaja

Favorite Songs

Aretha Franklin- *I Came To Lift Him Up*

Tasha Cobbs Leonard- *This Is A Move*

Shania Wilson- *Never Be The Same*

The Impressions- *Keep On Pushing*

K.C. and Sunshine Band- *Boogie Shoes*

Day 18

LIVING YOUR KINGDOM LIFE UNAPOLOGETICALLY

From this moment on living your life unapologetically, being unafraid of who you are called to be, and unafraid to use your gift(s) as God so leads you should be the top priority on YOUR accomplishments list. Always remember YOU will not get another one in this lifetime.

Day eighteen is significant as prophetically it means life, the welfare of humanity, and building something of lasting benefit. When broken down in its simplest form, nine (1+8), it represents birth. Since you have stayed the course the last seventeen days of this beautiful journey intended to cultivate you to a better you, unapologetically this time around, adjust your mind and see it's time to give birth to your calling by activating your gifts. As you are being birthed into who God chose you to be, understand this birthing comes with a new level of confidence. It comes with a new level of understanding and knowledge. While it still comes with making mistakes, those mistakes keep you humble and at the feet of JESUS praying for guidance. Furthermore, it is proof you are trying. You have been brave enough to take this journey. You're making everyday count by spending immeasurable time alone with God in fellowship getting to know Him and the majesty of His power in your life.

Who do you know living their kingdom life unapologetically? My thoughts bring me to Prophetess Juanita Bynum. Seeing her from her humble beginnings to watching the rise, fall, and rise again of her ministry is truly God showing us how to go through to get to. Many of us either watched or heard her testimony.

From having a nervous breakdown, to living on welfare, going through a public divorce, her name being scandalized among other Pastors, failed relationships, and even her ministry taking a fall, to God raising her back up again. Despite the trials Prophetess Bynum endured, she stayed the course. She continued walking in her kingdom authority, praying, fasting, and teaching the word of God, allowing HIM to restore her to living her kingdom life unapologetically. Beloved it is the anointing which destroys the yoke of bondage.

Wherever your gift(s) lead you, live your life unapologetically unto God. Take the masks off and be your authentic self despite your shortcomings. You have been forgiven and Jesus cast your sins into the sea of forgetfulness. There is never a need to retreat when people try to remind you of their memories of you. Continue going forth Focusing 2 Finish on your God given assignments. Keep your cap and gown in your view for graduation day will surely come for you. There is nothing on this earth in comparison to the value of living your Kingdom life unapologetically!!!

As we end this beautiful day of blessings, answer three simple questions:

1. Are you living your kingdom life unapologetically? If not, what's holding you back?
2. What does living your kingdom life unapologetically looks like?
3. How will you live your kingdom life unapologetically moving forward?

<u>Scriptures</u>

On the day I called, You answered me; And you made me bold and confident with renewed strength in my life. (Psalm 138:3 KJV)

This is the remarkable degree of confidence which we as believers are entitled to have before Him: that if we ask anything according to His will that is consistent with His plan and purpose, He hears us. And if we know for a fact, as indeed we do that He hears and listens to us whatever we ask, we also know with settled and absolute knowledge that we have granted to us the requests which we have asked from Him. (1 John 5:14-15 KJV)

Thou wilt shew me; the path of life. In thy presence is fullness of joy, at thy right hand there are pleasures evermore. (Psalm 16:11 KJV)

So teach us to number our days, that we may apply our hearts unto wisdom. Return, O LORD, how long? And let it repent thee concerning thy servants. O satisfy us early with thy mercy that we may rejoice and be glad all our days. Make us glad according to the days wherein thou hast afflicted us and the years wherein we have seen evil. Let thy work appear unto thy servants, and thy glory unto their children. And let the beauty of the LORD our God be upon us and establish thou the work of our hands upon us; yea, the work of our hands establish thou it. (Psalm 90:12-17 KJV)

Then spake JESUS again unto them, saying I am the light of the world: he that followeth me shall not walk in darkness, but shall have the light of life. (John 8:12 KJV)

Famous Quote

"Somebody should tell us, right at the start of our lives that we are dying. Then we might live life to the limit, every minute, of every day. Do it! I say. Whatever you want to do, do it now! There are only so many tomorrows."

Pope Paul VI

Favorite Songs

Earnest Pugh-*Thank You*

Shania Wilson-Williams- *Never Be The Same*

TaRanda- *He's Been Faithful*

Shania Twain- *From This Moment On*

Elton John, Gladys Knight, Dionne Warwick & Stevie Wonder- *That's What Friends Are For*

Day 19

ANCHORED IN SELF-CARE & SELF-LOVE

YOUR RACE

Have you ever watched a track race whether during the Olympics or during the Track and Field season? If you have, have you ever noticed the last leg of each relay race. They are known as the anchor leg. The anchor leg is the one who has the most strength, is the fastest, and has the most experience. They carry the team to the finish line, making up potentially lost time to ensure the team finishes strong. Guess what? Day 19 is the day of the anchor as you prepare for the final leg of this part of your journey.

Self-love is regards to one's own well-being and happiness chiefly associated as a desirable rather than narcissistic characteristic. Self-love is imperative in order for you to stay anchored on this journey. Self-care is needed for you to detox for there to be a healthy balance of pouring out and receiving. You must take time for yourself to replenish your mind, body, and spirit allowing your cup to be refilled. When there is a calling upon your life to help others, whether you are a teacher, doctor, maintenance worker, Pastor, parent, or a spouse, in any capacity for which you are leading others, it can be draining. You will have to cultivate those whom you have been leading to pull from what they've been taught, trusting themselves to make the right decisions, so as to not overpour when there are those being sent who need your gift in a fresh manner. Self-care is being honest with yourself in knowing when to pour and when not to pour. It's knowing when you are drained and knowing how to inform others around you of the need for rest. Some healthy examples of self-care to free your mind are:

- Sign up for a dance class.
- Take a trip to the beach or to the mountains.
- Pamper yourself day at the spa.
- Read your favorite book.
- Take a short road trip.
- Turn off your phone, take no calls or appointments, set aside a day or two just for you.

The driving force to keep you from now on is self-care which leads to self-love. You must care and love oneself first and foremost as it influences every area of your life.

There was a time in my life I didn't give myself enough self-love trying to be there for everyone. If they called I was there. Whatever they needed me to do, I was there making sure they were happy, while at the same time I was miserable and running on empty. Yet I still put my best foot forward with a smile. I got to a point of realizing I had to take care of me and God's business. I couldn't take care of HIS business being everything to everyone, being a people pleaser, but not self-pleasing. People said I became arrogant, but that was not the case. I was understanding and activating self-love. I reached my place of peace and began focusing to finish the race given to me in order to complete the work I must answer for. It was not me disregarding people's feelings or seeking admiration or entitlement, I understood the importance of self-care when being chosen by God and walking out the assignment upon my life. Some understood, while others didn't. Be prepared. You will experience the same.

Despite all that, when I truly came to the realization of my purpose in the world, an anchor runner to the tribe I've been called to, my Focusing 2 Finish race drastically changed. I set aside two days weekly where I implement self-care. If requests from others do not align with the scheduled plans for the week, I kindly say no. Saying yes takes me off track of what needs to be completed. I take a day monthly to pamper myself and eat alone at my favorite restaurant without carrying the cares of everyone else on my shoulders. I always replenish myself daily with positive affirmations. Self-care and self- love are the refusal to give in to defeat and not complete your life's race. You must stay anchored in what is beneficial for your mind, body, and spirit. Allow me to leave you with some examples of self-love:

- Setting healthy boundaries.

- Being true to yourself.
- Giving yourself a break from self judgement
- Speaking kind and powerful words about yourself
- Being intentional
- Being YOU!

These examples will help keep your mental state good, spirit health good, and keep you rooted and grounded in this race living a joyful life. It's going to ensure you're a balanced vessel full of self- assurance, self- confidence, and self-care. Most importantly self-love will give you great strength and the wisdom of endurance to remain steadfast and immovable. YOU are the anchor leg selected for this amazing race. You are approaching the finish line on this journey God has begun in you.

As you continue this journey, keep sticky notes of positive affirmations in your most frequently visited places to ensure you are putting you first. Everything starts with you making a conscious decision of honoring who you are in every way knowing your oil (gift) is too expensive and time is too valuable to waste. Therefore, nourishment is necessary. Staying anchored with self-care works hand in hand with self-love. It keeps you grounded while it builds your confidence. Because of your love and appreciation of the gift(s) gifted to you, love Him and yourself enough to endure the race by ensuring you are honoring the gift of self-love and self-care.

Scriptures

This hope is a strong and trustworthy anchor for our souls. It leads us through the curtain into God's inner sanctuary. (Hebrews 6:19 KJV)

Therefore, my beloved brethren, be ye steadfast, immovable, always abounding in the work of the Lord, knowing your labor is not in vain in the Lord. (1 Corinthians 15:58 KJV)

Therefore, since we are surrounded by such a great cloud of witnesses, let us throw off everything that hinders and the sin that so easily entangles. And let us run with perseverance the race marked out for us. (Hebrews 12:1 KJV)

Being confident of this very thing, that he which hath begun a good work in you will perform it until the day of Jesus Christ (Philippians 1:6 KJV)

Famous Quote

"When you love yourself you tell yourself you love yourself, you don't ask others what they think, you congratulate yourself."

Miles Monroe

Favorite Songs

Holly Star-*Run The Race*

Douglas Miller- *My Soul Has Been Anchored*

Loony- *Some Kind Of Love*

CeCe Winans- *Blessed Assurance*

I Am A Disciple- *Running The Race*

Fantasia Barrino- *The Lord Is Blessing Me*

Patti LaBelle- *New Attitude*

Day 20

Serving The Nations Gratitude

OPENED DOORS

As you embark upon your journey of being sent to the nations, I don't know how your shout will be, nor the songs you will sing, but look at it as having just won the world's largest lottery to ever be seen. Your gift(s) are priceless and so is the impact you will make, but do not forget the main reason you are here and who got you here. As a written promise your gift(s) will make room for you. They are going to open doors for you to access nations. Nations within your community, church, child's school, your job, and even social media. You'll have access to talk and meet people all over the world. We all will not travel abroad, but as we coexist with people from different parts of the world the journey will be so beautiful.

This is your day of thanksgiving to the most high God. You were bought with a price, chosen, and entrusted to shift nations. This is a time to be grateful because the place you are in now is no comparison of what is about to occur in your life. The people you will meet, the places you will go, and most importantly the lives you will help transform for the glory of God is priceless. Take a few moments to bestow gratitude for all you have experienced and received, for those individuals whom God has put in your path to shift their lives using the gifts He's entrusted you with. In order to go and serve among many nations you must always have the spirit and mindset of gratitude. People do not have to receive you nor your gifts. Be thankful you have been favored of the Lord to make a lifelong impact in this world.

I am forever thankful to the people who granted me opportunities to interview celebrities on the red carpet. They include Mrs. Ebony Porter-Ike, President of Epi-Media Group, Kimberly Chapman, Co- Founder of Sheen Magazine, Pastor Sammie Haynes,, Founder of Love Freedom Movement, Prince Carter, President of Global Line Media Group, LLC,

Jerome Dorn, Founder of InDaHouseMedia/News Company, Evangelist Beverly Broadus Green (Snoop Dogg's Mother), and 108 Praise Radio. Each of these opportunities grew into lifelong relationships and opportunities of being able to serve. They were opportunities where my gifts opened doors and brought me before great men and women. When you have been given such opportunities, the key is to remain humble. In the access I was granted I remained humbled with a spirit of gratitude in all things. Great people will enter your life. They will expect you to be trustworthy, integral, and compassionate. Not having these characteristics will quickly close doors of access.

As you are being called to the nations, exemplify the spirit of gratitude. Always thank GOD first and foremost. Thank those who granted you opportunities. Pay it forward by volunteering your service. Give compassion as it generates an energy of kindness. Having these principles will allow you and others to lead fulfilling lives. When you learn to remain humble and trustworthy, not only will you receive the same thing in return, it will continue to open doors for you. As you continue to serve do it with joy and a heart of gratitude.

Start a gratitude journal with these five questions:

- How do you show gratitude?
- What nation(s) have you been chosen to serve?
- Who gave you an opportunity to serve?
- Who and what are you grateful for?
- When will you begin to pay it forward?

Scriptures

Go ye therefore and teach all nations baptizing them in the name of the Father, and of the Son, and of the Holy Spirit. Teaching them to observe all things whatsoever I have commanded of you, and lo, I am with you always, even unto the end of the world. Amen (Matthew 28:19-20 KJV)

Let the word of Christ dwell in you richly, teaching and admonishing one another in all wisdom, singing psalms, and spiritual songs, singing with grace in your hearts to the Lord. (Colossians 3:16 KJV)

Make a joyful noise unto the Lord all ye lands. Serve the Lord with gladness come before his presence with singing. Know ye that the Lord is God it is he that hath made us, and not we ourselves, we are his people, and the sheep of his pasture. Enter into his gates with thanksgiving, and into his courts with praise be thankful unto him and bless his name. For the Lord is good; and his truth endureth to all generations. (Psalms 100 KJV)

Give praise to the LORD, proclaim his name; make known among the nations what he has done. Sing to him, sing praise to him; tell of his wonderful acts. Glory in his holy name; let the hearts of those who seek the LORD rejoice. Look to the LORD and his strength; seek his face always. Remember the wonders he has done, his miracles, and the judgements he pronounced. You his servants, the descendants of Israel, his chosen ones, the children of Jacob. (1 Chronicles 16:8-13 KJV)

Famous Quote

"Thankfulness is the beginning of gratitude. Gratitude is the completion of thankfulness. Thankfulness may consist merely of words. Gratitude is shown in acts."

Henri Frederic Amiel

Favorite Songs

Shirley Caesar- *Go*

Zach Williams-*Old Church Choir*

Tamela Mann- *Praise Medley (Live)*

Marcia Griffiths- *Electric Slide*

Cupid- *Cupid Shuffle*

Day 21

Purpose, Not Performance

RACE WON!!

Now that you have come to the end of this twenty-one day journey, understand everything you have learned was for your purpose and not for you to go out and perform. The goal is to be purposeful in your gifts. How does it feel finishing and winning the race for this part of your Focusing 2 Finish journey? The hurdles you could not cross before are finally gone and you have a new start. You are now free to walk boldly and humbly in your Kingdom Purpose. You did it knowing your existence here on earth is greater than fulfilling your own personal happiness. Performance was not the reason you completed the race. It was the hunger of being filled for the overflow in your life.

I remember being at the Martin Luther King, Jr. Celebration when the next generations of leaders were being passed the baton of leadership by Mrs. Leila Walker. Mrs. Walker was a phenomenal woman known as the songbird of the south, who marched with Dr. Martin Luther King, Jr. Lelia Walker's Martin Luther King, Jr. Celebration is an event held for the community to celebrate and give back to families. Her purpose was to continuously encourage the community to use the power of their voice by voting. She also empowered them to preserve the same opportunities for the generations coming after her to stand together for equality for affordable housing, community centers for the youth, fair pay and jobs for the city, and social justice for everyone in the deep south of Sylvester Georgia. Mrs. Walker stated she'd served her time and her footsteps were getting shorter. Therefore, while she still had time left to see the legacy be carried out for many years, it was time to pass the baton to the younger generation. Mrs. Walker was also a political activist who encouraged people to vote in Sylvester, Georgia. She was later inducted into The Black Women Hall of Fame. What an honor it was to watch the baton be passed and proudly accepted by the next generation of leaders.

Your assignment has a never-ending purpose. Mrs. Walker is an example that your race will continue even after you have passed the baton to the next runner. There will always be someone you will have to teach, train, and provide strategies to on continuing to run their race. As you have completed this part of your race today with purpose and being a winner, continue to be a better YOU for God's glory, not performing for an outside show to the world. Just the same as you have finished with power, strength, and endurance, know YOU are blessed to be a blessing, Jesus' hands are upon you, and your territory is enlarged indeed. Now walk in God's favor. It's yours for the asking because you made yourself available to be a track star, gaining wisdom, knowledge, and understanding of who you have been created, called, and chosen to be for God's Glory. Remember it is neither about you nor the situations. Whether you have been working a long time sharing your gift(s) or just getting started, enjoy the journey and stay the course.

GLORY HALLELUJAH! INCREASE! RACE WON!!!

<u>Scriptures</u>

I have fought a good fight, I have finished my course, I have kept the faith. (2 Timothy 4:7 KJV)

Therefore, since we are surrounded by such a great cloud of witnesses let us throw off everything that hinders and the sin that so easily entangles. And let us run with perseverance the race marked out for us, fixing our eyes on Jesus, the pioneer and perfecter of our faith. For the joy set before him he endured the cross, scorning its shame, and sat down at the right hand of the throne of God. Consider him who endured such opposition from sinners, so that you will not grow weary and lost heart. (Hebrews 12:1 KJV)

Do you not know in a race all the runners run, but only one gets the prize? Run in such a way as to get the prize. Everyone who competes in the games goes into strict training. They do it to get a crown that will not last, but we do it to get a crown that will not last, but we do it to get a crown that will last forever. Therefore, I do not run like someone running aimlessly, do not fight like a boxer beating the air.

No, I strike a blow to my body and make it my slave so that after I have preached to others, I myself will not be disqualified for the prize. (1 Corinthians 9:24-25 KJV)

You need to preserve so that when you have done the will of God, you will receive what he has promised. (Hebrews 10:36 KJV)

But none of these things move me, neither count I my life dear unto myself, so that I might finish my course with joy, and the ministry, which I have received of the Lord Jesus, to testify the gospel of the grace of God. (Acts 20:24 KJV)

That ye might walk worthy of the Lord unto all pleasing, being fruitful in every good work, increasing in the knowledge of God; For this cause we also the day we heard it, do not cease to pray for you, and to desire that ye might be filled with the knowledge of his will in all wisdom and spiritual understanding. That ye might walk worthy of the Lord unto all pleasing, being fruitful in every good work, and increasing in the knowledge of God; Strengthened with all might, according, to his glorious power, unto all patience and long suffering with joyfulness. Giving thanks unto the Father, which hath made us, meet the partakers of the inheritance of the saints in light. (Colossians 1:9-12 KJV)

Famous Quote

"Don't be afraid, Be focused, Be determined Be hopeful, Be empowered."

Michelle Obama

Favorite Songs

William Murphy- *Your Love*

Mary Mary- *Shackles*

Smokie Norful- *Dear God (Live)*

Donald Lawrence and the Tri City Singers- *Bless Me (The Prayer of Jabez)*

Bishop Paul S. Morton- *Never Be Bound Again*

Casey J- *Fill Me Up*

Pharrell Williams- *Happy*

Lois Lane- *Chinese Checkers*

Deitrick Haddon- *Well Done*

You have completed the purpose surrounding this book which was to help you get to your destiny of Focusing 2 Finish what God has planned for you. Because many of us are multi-gifted, I encourage you to take a Spiritual Gifts test that can be found at https://mintools.com/spiritual-gifts-test.htm. This test will help you differentiate the dynamics of your gifts. It will also allow you to know your top three to five gifts. Take a moment now to take the spiritual gift test mentioned in order for you to be able to further understand where God is calling you. Once you understand and discover your gift(s), you'll be better equipped with a clear sense of your never ending mission. You will pass the baton to the one destined to carry it out. They will model the characteristics of a Kingdom minded person. They'll be excited to be connected to one who will extend the attributes of humbleness, along with being loving and merciful towards them and others.

Whenever I find myself being frustrated when things seem as if they are not coming together, these are some of my favorite affirmations given by some of the WORLD'S GREATEST and ANOINTED people. Some I know personally. They helped me keep it together by having me to refocus, take a deep breath, press onward, and recite some POWERFUL WORDS given to me along this life's journey. Others I have either heard during an interview or written in archives.

Evangelist Beverly Broadus Green

Celebrity Mom, Inspirational Speaker, Actress, Snoop-Dogg's Mother

- If I can change my thoughts I can change anything. Today, I will make progress toward my goals. My thoughts do not control me, I control my thoughts. I am capable of what I am willing to work for. I trust myself and instincts above anyone else. To love myself is the ultimate love. To make small steps towards big goals is progress. There is no greater goal than being content with yourself. No one controls how I feel about myself, but me.
- Remember this: YOU have enough, YOU do enough, and most importantly, YOU are enough.

Mrs. Kimberly M. Chapman

Sheen Magazine Publisher

- You don't need a title to be a leader. YOU lead by example.
- Confidence has no competition. Stay positive, work hard, and make it happen.

Ms. JosCynthia Mason

Celebrity Award Winning Multicultural Hairstylist and Educator

- I realized I don't have to doubt how far I can go. I just have to remember how far I have come, everything I've faced, all the battles I've won, and all the fears I've overcome.
- You have three choices in life: Give up, give in, or give it all you've got.

Ms. Patrina Anderson

Albany State University Facilities Assistant Director

- You can like someone. You may even love someone. But you may have to leave someone for peace.
- BUT GOD!!!

Miss Chelsea Patel

My Beautiful, Brilliant, Courageous, Loving, Phenomenal Daughter

- We do not need magic to transform our world. We carry all the power we need inside ourselves already. -J.K Rowling
- Your life is already a miracle of chance waiting for you to shape its destiny. -Toni Morrison

Ms. Nikki Nycole

Celebrity Radio Personality, T.V. Host, Actress, Producer, Writer

- Your cup will overflow; we're in the overflow sister.
- That's Our Connection.

Ms. LeAnn Foster

Celebrity Radio/Media Personality- Loving LeAnn, Domestic Violence Advocate, Inspirational Speaker

- I am deserving of all I desire.
- Sight is a function of the eyes. Vision is a function of the heart. (Dr. Myles Munroe)

Mrs. Robbie Ray

Celebrity Radio/ Media Personality, Producer, Actor, Brand Strategist, Executive Director

- You have a special gift and you must minister to the world.
- I don't know if you are holding back. Only you know what you have to do, and you must do it.

Mr. D'vante Black

5X Grammy Nominated Mastering Engineer, Music Coordinator

- Those who win big do it not by fighting over what's already there, but by creating something that has never existed before.
- In good times or bad, in easy or challenging circumstances, what matters most is what you do next. You can always make that something great.

Mr. Jamal Webb

Educator, Minister, Actor, Model, Husband, Father, Bethune Cookman Graduate

- My name is VICTORY!!!
- Erase the mistakes of my PAST. Guide the steps of my PRESENT. Bless the DAYS of my FUTURE.

I pray as you continue your journey, every word written out of the oracles of GOD through myself along with others and I add value to YOUR life.

Below add your favorite affirmations. Speak and believe them daily. Our prayer is for you to complete every assignment written in the plans for your life and receive your CROWN OF GLORY. Last, but not least, the question is, "As you are traveling this world and when you are long gone, what do YOU want YOUR legacy to say?"

1._____

2._____

3._____

4._____

5._____

6._____

7._____

8._____

9._____

10._____

11._____

12._____

13._____

14._____

15._____

16._____

17._____

18._____

19._____

20._____

21._____

Music is a balm in Gilead for me. Whether it is spiritual or secular, it's the beauty of God's amazing gifts He has given to so many people to uplift our souls. Being given the opportunity daily to go in God's presence with singing is truly a blessing. It lets Him know how much we love Him. Nevertheless, I believe God has a great sense of humor. Reason being, the musical gifts He gives to artist who sing gospel, secular, love, country, R&B, rap, jazz, classical, etc. I love them all. Give me a good line dance song so Jesus, the Angels, and I can dance. Maybe some of the songs listed in this masterpiece may not resonate with your spirit. Make your playlist and enjoy every given moment praising, singing, and dancing unto the Most High God.

1._____

2._____

3._____

4._____

5._____

6._____

7._____

8._____

9._____

10._____

11._____

12._____

13._____

14._____

15._____

16._____

17._____

18._____

19._____

20._____

21.

PLAYLIST OF MUSIC I LEAVE WITH YOU

We all know music is the Balm in Gilead. On our best days, as well as our worst days, it calms, heals, relaxes, and lifts your spirit, along with setting the atmosphere. Music has always brought me hope and power in whatever situation I was going through.

In this twenty-one day MASTERPIECE, all genres of music have been shared. From Gospel to R&B, Country, Jazz, and Classical. I hope this music brings you enjoyment throughout your reading along with the playlist you created above. As the cliché says "Dance as though no one is watching. Love as though you've never been hurt. Sing as though no one can hear you. Live as though heaven is on earth. I hope you dance, love, sing, and live who you have been CALLED, CREATED, and CHOSEN to be without no regrets, sharing YOUR journey with loved ones, friends, people you meet along the way, and the ones who are assigned to YOUR destiny. GOD BLESS!!!

1. *Waymaker-* Darlene Zschech & William McDowell I REVERE (Official Live Video)
2. *How Deeply I Need You-* Shekinah Glory Ministry
3. *Love's Medley-* Earth Wind & Fire
4. *You Are-* Charlie Wilson
5. *Jesus Take The Wheel-* Carrie Underwood
6. *Won't He Do It-* Featuring Roshon Fegan/ Koryn Hawthorne
7. *Grateful-* Hezekiah Walker & The Love Fellowship Crusade
8. *Sail Away-* Kenny Barron
9. *In A Mellow Tone-* Javon Jackson, Paul Gill, David Hazeltine, Tony Reedus
10. *You Still Love Me (LIVE)-* Tasha Cobbs Leonard
11. *Have Your Way (Feat. Jason Nelson)—* Casey J
12. *I Know I've Been Changed-* Carlton Pearson
13. *Wonderful World-* Otis Redding
14. *Center Of My Joy-* Ruben Studdard
15. *There Is A King In You-* Donald Lawrence
16. *Old Songs Medley-* Carlton Pearson
17. *How Great Is Our God/How Great Thou Art-* CeCe Winans
18. *I'll Take You There-* Staples Singers
19. *I'm Gonna Be Ready –* Yolanda Adams
20. *He Still Loves Me-* Beyonce and Walter Williams

21. *Still Say, Thank You*- Smokie Norful
22. *Your Presence Is A Gift*- Pastor E. Dewey Smith
23. *No Ordinary Worship*- Kelontae Gavin
24. *Heaven*- Mary, Mary

Made in the USA
Middletown, DE
28 February 2023